Slop Chest

A Comprehensive View of Rigging the
Topsail Schooner *Shenandoah*
Coupled with Random Anecdotes

D. Zachorne
Master in Sail

**Slop Chest: A Comprehensive View
of Rigging the Topsail Schooner Shenandoah
Coupled with Random Anecdotes**

Copyright © 2020 D. Zachorne

Produced and printed
by Stillwater River Publications.
All rights reserved. Written and produced in the
United States of America. This book may not be reproduced
or sold in any form without the expressed, written
permission of the author and publisher.

Visit our website at
www.StillwaterPress.com
for more information.

First Stillwater River Publications Edition
Library of Congress Control Number: 2020917554
Paperback ISBN: 978-1-952521-51-5
Hardcover ISBN: 978-1-952521-62-1

1 2 3 4 5 6 7 8 9 10

Written by Dominic Zachorne
Published by Stillwater River Publications,

Pawtucket, RI, USA.

Publisher's Cataloging-In-Publication Data
(Prepared by The Donohue Group, Inc.)
Names: Zachorne, D. (Dominic), author.
Title: Slop chest : a comprehensive view of rigging the topsail
schooner Shenandoah coupled with random anecdotes / D. Zachorne,
Master in Sail.
Description: First Stillwater River Publications edition. | Pawtucket,
RI, USA : Stillwater River Publications, [2020]
Identifiers: ISBN 9781952521515 (paperback)
Subjects: LCSH: Schooners--United States. | Masts and rigging. |
Zachorne, Dominic--Career in sailing. | Sailing--Anecdotes.
Classification: LCC VM311.F7 Z33 2020 | DDC 623.822/3--dc23

To my parents George and "Mike" Zachorne,
my brother Christian, the Skipper,
ex-mates and crew of *Shenandoah*,
family and friends that have helped to mold my character,
thank you.
May your anchors hold fast.

Table of Contents

Preface

Over the years, I have read so many sea stories about everything from pirates to shipwrecks to arctic exploration. In these books, the authors tell about things like getting the light air sails or "old suit" off and bending on the storm suit or taking down yards. Unfortunately, they never explain the finer points of the work. It was just part of the routine of running the vessel, but what was the tackle to stretch a sail or used to lower a yard? This information is being lost as the technology and methods change. It is very much like what has happened to the motorist. With my parents' generation or my grandparents', a flat tire was an all-too-common occurrence. It was part of owning an automobile and driving. A driver had to learn what good equipment looked like, and to a small degree, how to care for and repair it. Now the flat is so rare that drivers can go for a lifetime and never have the experience of one.

Once or twice I have come across a passage or short story where someone got a job done, as in the book *On the Bottom* by Commander Edward Ellsberg. Whether it described a rigging job or how to handle a vessel, these tales have all captured my imagination. I recall one story where Richard Quick, captain of the *Edward Sewall*, had a coal fire in the hold which made the foremast settle. The ship had iron lower masts, and the heat from the fire made the iron soft. I cannot imagine being at sea in a four-masted bark and having the foremast settle. That must have scared the bejeezus out of everyone. Yet the crew got the vessel under control and sailed into San Francisco, where the crew derigged the vessel and repaired the bottom of the foremast. They then restepped the mast and rerigged the vessel, all without any help from a rigging company. The author covered the process but left out the finer details of the job. I am going to try and cover the finer details here in this book, with my experience on *Shenandoah* primarily, while relaying my own sea stories. I have never encountered a coal fire in the hold that made *Shenandoah's* foremast settle, but we did part a main peak halyard and replace it while under way.

The great wind ships have come to a time when the men who could so naturally and efficiently work their ropes and blocks have faded over the horizon. All this seamanship was once common knowledge among sailors, bosuns, mates and skippers, but now only a few keep it alive and even fewer pass it on to the next generation. Every once in a while I hear about an outfit that got some powder for their cannon and took on a job on their own. But for the most part seamanship has been regulated down to making knife lanyards and turks head bracelets. In my opinion, tying an overhand knot four different ways is not what I would call great seamanship; taking a 108 foot topsail schooner and club-hauling in Vineyard Haven Harbor to pick up a mooring is.

Part of seamanship's demise, I think, is all the synthetic fiber being used on our big wind ships now. This practice by itself removes the need for recognizing worn out gear, overhauling gear and exercising the practices of seamen. Then there's the fact that major parts of big jobs are being handled by "professional contractors" or "specialists." Don't get me wrong; there have always been professionals ashore, but they were not called upon to get yards down so a vessel could be dry docked or put away for the winter. There has become little need for real knowledge in the art of an old-time rigger aboard ships today. This has far-reaching effects, similar to the motorist not having the experience of a flat. The modern driver will lose the ability to handle a vehicle in odd conditions and be hampered in building knowledge about what safe equipment looks like.

I also no longer see the kind of partnering between an old timer and young apprentice that there once was. The young upstarts are trying to learn on their own without guidance, and, in some cases, they're making it up as they go. We have all heard or read things about crew doing jobs that are beyond their scope. I do not blame them for the damage they do, but myself and all like me for not doing our job in teaching them or being there to answer their questions. I have noticed some of these interested beginners have gone to the textbook or school, which is good and important, but in many cases they are full of theory that is taken as fact. There is no practical experience gained or passed on with these types of education, but the graduate gets a certificate and there they are! "Learned." Of course, this book may be construed as theory someday, but I hope it will be seen for what it is: one man's life experience.

Many of us, in our avocation or trade, have been shown or taught something from the previous generation which was taught from the previous generation, etc. In keeping this information alive and passing it along person to person, we are keeping alive a family tree of knowledge. For example, Bob Douglas being taught how to splice by Lambert Knight who was part of the crew on *Parma* in 1932 with Robert Conx and Alan Villers. My father working with "Unc Allen," Godfrey French Allen, who worked with Rod Stevens and Manuel Parece building wooden boats. Then there is my connection with history, growing up with Bill Church who was with Commander Edward Ellsberg on the Falcon when they dove on the S-4 sub off Block Island and sailed with Admiral Bird to the Antarctic. This continuum of knowledge is, in my opinion, the most valuable form of learning, as well as impressive. I say most valuable because it dissolves the theories of the textbook or school and builds on the most tried and practical methods of years of experience. I say impressive because, for me, it's a wonderful memory that a man like "The Admiral" – Rear Admiral Edwin M. Rosenberg – took the time to teach me some boat handling skills when I was a young boy in Virginia at Glass Marine.

Over the years I have tried to pass along what I have learned and with it, once or twice, an artifact. Someday my wire splicing vise, which was given to me by Eddy Gamage, Harvey Gamage's nephew, and belonged to Henry Bhondell, will need a new custodian. I have always felt it is my duty to keep this "family tree" growing and encourage the imagination of the young.

What I have put here in my "slop chest" to provide for future crews, bo'suns, mates and maybe even skippers of whatever vessel it may be aboard, does not pertain only to *Shenandoah*, but to any vessel that crosses a yard, carries a topmast, or flies a gaff. It mostly pertains to traditional vessels, but there are descriptions of blocks and tackle that may help the modern yachtsman or anyone trying to move a large object. It should not be looked at as some kind of authority, for I am no expert and there are many ways to do any one thing. This book is only a compilation of what has worked for me, using the experience of those I have known and learned from, coupled with my own efforts. It is an attempt to document and maybe entertain, but more importantly, to add one more link in the "family tree" of sea history

Introduction

I first saw *Shenandoah* in Vineyard Haven harbor on a summer day in 1972.

I was a 16-year-old cadet on the training schooner *Tabor Boy*. I had just finished furling the starboard half of *Tabor Boy's* large square foresail. It wasn't a very good job, and it looked like a large load of laundry spilling out of its bag, and I was sent back aloft to do a better job.

I wanted to do a better job, and went to work on it. I had grown up reading C.S. Forrester's novels of British sailing warships during the Age of Sail, how the Royal Navy ruled the seas through excellence in seamanship. I learned how the ships could use their square topsails to maneuver, slow down, or even go backwards. But not in today's age. Even on the schooner *Tabor Boy*, we entered harbor and anchored under engine.

Just then *Shenandoah* came sailing into the harbor under full sail. She was beautiful, tall, graceful, and strong. Her great size flowed easily through the water as she approached her mooring in the crowded anchorage. I stared in awe of her lofty rig, its perfect proportions, and her trim topsails, which could sail close-hauled so well. I was hoping I would get to see her back her topsails to slow herself, as I had so often read about.

And she did. Her foreyards swung quickly round as she backed the fore tops'ls to check her way and she came to a stop and picked up her mooring, without any noise or fuss.

Then a young seaman went quickly aloft, laid out on her yards, and furled her tops'l and t'gallant quickly. The sails were so tight and neat that they looked like a little cap of snow on her yards. I looked at that and then back at my load of laundry, and said to myself, "Someday…"

In talking with Dominic years later, he told me, "I only heard of one time when she actually backed her tops'ls to pick up her mooring, sometime in the early seventies." Sometimes you get a whole lot of luck in ione little moment.

The world owes a debt of gratitude for this book. It preserves an important element of an age, a way of life, the beautiful ships, and the skills to sail them. While we have preserved historical ships like the *Constitution* and the *Victory*, and many museums to document the equipment, clothing, culture, and even the songs of that great era, the skills themselves are the most elusive and fragile, the hardest to record, the hardest to preserve. You can see the size and proportions of the sails, spars, and lines, but to know how to come about in a ship, and shift each sail with the right techniques in the right sequence, is the least recorded of all our maritime knowledge.

In this book Dominic has sought to record and preserve these skills, and has done it really well. Years later I did get to work as a seaman on Shenandoah and learned some of those skills, and I can attest that this book has preserved so much of them, in great detail, and with the greatest accuracy. Thank you, Dominic.

Theo Aschman

A Berth Forward of the Mast

My friend Captain Robert S. Douglas has for many years asked me to write down the different procedures and methods I've used in getting his vessel, *Shenandoah*, together in record time. He figures it would be like an instruction manual for the crew to use while rigging the schooner if I am not around to help. I have in the past done this halfheartedly and told Bob, "You've gotten along before I came along, you'll manage after I'm gone." I've since come to the realization it's more about the documentation of the schooner, but not being a writer, actually not being very literary at all, this has been difficult for me. In the past, I have written down small details for a project or two, but nothing of any real insight or consequence. Now with the fiftieth anniversary of *Shenandoah's* sailing season having been celebrated and so many of those

Captain Bob Douglas of the Schooner Shenandoah, *watching the set of the sails.*
(photo by Dan Urish)

years being part of my life, I have been thinking back on all the happy days I've spent on the schooner with my good friend Bob. There were so many projects we did. So many adventures; learning and growing, not to mention all those great new people with stories to tell that I got to meet and befriend. It is now time to tell a few sea stories of my own, and relay what I know about rigging a 108-foot topsail schooner, so....

My story starts a little while ago in the summer of 1982 when we—Ma, Dad, my brother and I—were on our summer cruise on our 1929 English cutter, *Ampelisca*. Every summer NormaJean, George, Christian, and I would provision *Ampelisca* and head out, cruising along the coast. This has been going on since I was born because my parents moved aboard when they got married and I have lived aboard my entire life. The summer of 1982 was not very different from any other year, except for where the cruise took us. For many years the cruise was to the west, toward Long Island Sound, or down south to the Chesapeake. This year it was to the east; Buzzards Bay, Vineyard, and Nantucket Sounds were our destinations. Of those years roaming around the coast, I can only remember bits and pieces. Although I voyaged to the eastern coast from Halifax to the British Virgin Islands and Bermuda before I was twenty, this cruise was special; it set in motion a chain of events that is still in play. This was the summer when my family met the Douglas family and secured a lasting friendship.

My folks had a tendency to come to a place and enjoy it for a spell before pushing on. So, at anchor in Tarpaulin Cove, enjoying the sun of the late day, Christian and I were playing on the housetop with Legos and paper boats, while Ma and Dad were in the cockpit doing their thing. Most of the time, Dad would be reading a book while Ma would be sewing, crocheting, or doing needlework of some kind or other. Here we were, anchored up under the lee of the old farmhouse with a southwest wind. As I write about it, I think how peaceful and perfect that place is, and the times I spent with Bob up at the house with Hoyma (Forbs) Chereau, or at the old cemetery or with old Height, his wife Barbara, and Bob. I've been back there hundreds of times since, and that perfection has yet to diminish.

Tranquility.

On this clear summer day Dad happened to notice, coming over the hill where the lighthouse stands, square sails, then headsails and a large head rig! It was like watching one of Ma's *Horatio Hornblower* movies. From around this headland came a ghost all in white from a time now gone by. It was cool! Even then, Christian and I were taken with big ships. Ma and Dad took every opportunity to get us aboard one to look around, and so we had an appreciation for them.

I can only imagine what my dad was thinking when she started to take in her topsails, then her headsails, and come around to anchor in the middle of the cove. I had no idea there was a day coming when I was going to be the one paying out the chain on that starboard anchor. Dad watched with the glasses the whole time. He had her name as soon as her nose was around the bluff. That, followed by an entire history of where built, who owned her, and so on. Dad is like a walking encyclopedia or history book. As Dad was looking *Shenandoah* over and watching the crew up on the yards stowing the sails, we saw a Whitehall boat lowered and men tumbling into it. In due time it pulled up alongside us, with an older man aft, steering, and two boys at the oars.

They were invited aboard and the Whitehall was put astern. I remember Dad talking nonstop with a man who turned out to be the captain of the schooner, Captain Douglas, about boats while Ma served tea and snacks. Robbie and Jamie, who were the Captain's older boys, played with Christian and me on the cabin top in the sun with our paper boats. After some time of boat talk, Captain Douglas invited us for dinner aboard *Shenandoah*, and we all boarded *Shenandoah's* Whitehall and rowed back to the schooner. Robbie and Jamie took Christian and me around the vessel, and Captain Douglas showed Ma and Dad around. Christian and I were on a tall ship, and it was huge, with blocks equal to our two heads put together and ropes as big as our arms. Well, that was how it seemed to my brother and I, who were only the ripe old age of six and nine. Now, after thirty-six years of knowing that schooner, it does not seem as massive as it did that first time I walked the deck, though she is no less impressive.

In '89 *Ampelisca* was again on a summer cruise and met up with *Shenandoah* in Buzzards Bay. Bob was on a week's cruise with a group of adult passengers. We were invited aboard for a gam, dinner, and music by Bill Schustik. After, when we got home to *Ampelisca*, I asked my folks how one would go about getting on a vessel like *Shenandoah*. Dad said to just ask the captain for a berth forward of the mast. The next day we parted ways with *Shenandoah* and agreed to meet up at the end of the week in Vineyard Haven. That weekend we hung out with Bob on the waterfront, and it came up that he had some crew going back to school and was going to be shorthanded on the schooner. I thought it was my opportunity to ask if I could fill one of the berths, but Bob beat me to asking. A bit shocked, I asked if I could sleep on it and said I had to talk it over with my folks.

My folks are great. They, of course, had no problem with me spending some time on the schooner and said, "It'll do ya some good." Come the next day, I met up with Bob and told him I would take a bunk forward of the mast. It was midseason and he did not need me yet, so we made arrangements for me to crew on *Shenandoah* in two weeks. Bob went off on another week's cruise, and I went with my folks and Christian for a couple more weeks of sailing aboard *Ampelisca*. At first I was really excited, but as the time came for me to pack my bag and fulfill my obligation, I suffered from a severe case of cold feet. *Shenandoah* was so big and so mysterious I felt as though I was making a mistake. Ma and Dad said I couldn't turn back now, for I had given a man my word that I would be there to do a job and we had shaken on it. That was the hard part, knowing I had shook on it. They also said he was counting on me to be a part of his crew. Ma, in her infinite wisdom, said, "It's just another boat, pointy end, square end," and Dad said, "Yeah, it's just another voyage, out and back."

So the time came for me to pack my bag and board *Shenandoah*. Dad had worked the cruise so we ended in Woods Hole at the end of two weeks, where I took the ferry over to the Vineyard. Ma and Dad will say, "We had to pry his fingers off the rail," and I can't say that I was happy about going. I did pull myself together by the time I got to Vineyard Haven. *Shenandoah* was up against the Coastwise Wharf, with the crew on the paint barge touching up her topsides. I introduced myself to the mate, and he put me to work.

Shenandoah was finishing up her twenty-fifth summer, and all was done very showy and proper. The crew were older and took pride in their work. They were hyped up and excited over twenty-five years of the schooner sailing as well. I sure did enjoy working with them that summer.

Riding the Islander *to Vineyard Haven.*

For me, that first season was one hell of an experience. I never would have guessed I would still be at it today after twenty-nine years. Many of the blocks on the boat were as big as my head, which has not changed, and the rope was close to the diameter of my wrists. About the only thing I could lift by myself was a plate, which for the most part was what I did. Being the new kid on board, I was thrown in the galley as "Peggy," a term used by Shackleton for his galley boy or cook's helper.

The cook that year was Joe, a friend of mine now, but then he was a miserable man to work for. He would dirty every dish he could get his hands on. We, the crew, used to call him "Greasy Joe." I cannot say Joe was ever too hard on me. Actually, he started my guitar-playing career, but it did not last.

I never became a rock star. Joe is, and has, many records out there in the world. When my "Peggy" duties were taken care of I could work the deck with the rest of the crew, pulling on lines and furling sail. This is what was cool for me, though I do enjoy cooking.

Now, I have spent a lifetime pulling on lines and furling sail on all kinds of boats, but *Shenandoah* is not any kind of boat. *Shenandoah* is big, everything about her: sails, anchors, and spars. She is very overbuilt compared to other vessels her size. It takes teamwork to make *Shenandoah* "go where you want her to go, not necessarily where she wants to go" (Irving Johnson). Everything on *Shenandoah* is done by hand; no donkey engine, hydraulics, or electric winches as on many other vessels of today or the past. It takes knowledge and sometimes brute force to get jobs done, because the only horsepower is "Norwegian steam," as Charlie Barr, who considered Norwegians the best sailors and employed only them on his yachts, called it.

Well, the end of my trick was just about up when the captain asked me if I could spend another three weeks helping with downrigging the vessel. He said the crew was bailing on him and he was left with the mate and bo'sun. At this point my whole outlook had changed, and on the phone I told my folks how Bob needed me to help out. Back home, school was going to be starting, but my folks thought my tour on the schooner was a better education and figured missing two weeks was no big deal. Of course I didn't get anything but encouragement from them, and one hell of a yarn to tell. I hope you get as much of a kick out of reading about it as I did living it.

"Standard Takeoff"

WHILE I RAN THE DECK OF *SHENANDOAH* AS HER MATE, I made sure all in the crew could do any of the jobs on deck. I have always seen myself as a teacher while working the deck of *Shenandoah*. The lessons included handling the anchor chain and anchors, which is generally the mate's job only, one of few that is specific to one person. Bob was never comfortable with this and I understood why, but I felt this was important, because you never know when someone may become unable to do his or her job. These vessels are school ships after all, and it gave everyone a broader education about what was happening on the vessel and eliminated risk of any favoritism. In addition, it spawned respect for difficult tasks and rank. Most importantly, it amplified the education of the crew as a whole and gave the next mate or bo'sun the opportunity to get their feet wet before they were put on the spot. This experience was something I never got.

To get *Shenandoah* underway there's a fair bit of preparation. In a standard takeoff, the mains'l and fores'l are gotten on before one starts taking in the anchor chain, although I have been aboard when a flake or flake-and-a-half of chain are taken in before the mains'l and fores'l are set. This is because there may be a lot of chain out and/or a lot of wind, so having sail off reduces the windage on the vessel. This, in turn, reduces pressure on the chain and windlass, making it much easier to shorten up on the scope.

"Let's get her underway," is the word from the skipper. "Standard takeoff, Mr. Mate. Stays'l to starboard." The mate would yell out, "Stand by your mains'l, sing out when you're ready on the peak and throat." This would let everyone on the schooner know that the mains'l was going to be raised and we were going sailing. Four of the crew, two per halyard, would take up the halyards and direct the passengers to even themselves up along the rails, taking in hand the peak or throat halyards. The throat is led off to the port side of the vessel with the peak on the starboard side. If we were doing day sails, we would cancel the sail if less than fourteen people signed up. Less than seven per halyard or yawl boat fall makes for a hard pull. In the early nineties, Bob gave up on adult passengers and shifted over to schoolchildren from the fifth and sixth grades. There was quite a bit of talk over whether the little people could do the work of getting sail on. I myself had my doubts, but with Bill Schustik and his sea chanteys on board, there was no question about it. The kids can outwork the adults.

Anyway, the rest of the crew would work toward getting the schooner ready for sail by stretching out the stays'l and reeving her sheets, then stretching the downhauls for the inner and outer jibs, as well as letting go of the gaskets on these sails. If conditions were favorable, the gaskets for the tops'l and t'gallant would be let go as well. As for the crew on the main peak and throat halyards, one of them, generally the guy at the head of the line, would sing out, "Ready on peak," or, "Ready on throat," depending on who was ready first. Once they both sang out the mate would yell out, "Go ahead together." This would prompt Bill, if he was on board, to start in on one of his sea chanteys.

They call me hanging Johnny,
Away, boys, away!
They say I hang for money!
So hang, boys, hang down!

They say I hanged my mother,
My sisters and my brothers

They say I hanged my granny,
I strung her up so canny

They say I hung a copper,
I gave him the long dropper

I'd hang the mates and skippers,
I'd hang 'em by their flippers

A rope, a beam, a ladder,
I'll hang ye all together

Hang `em from the yardarm,
Hang the sea and buy a pig farm

They say I hang for money,
Hanging ain't bloody funny

They call me hanging Johnny,
Ain't never hanged nobody

The man at the head of the peak halyard is supposed to keep an eye on the gaff and try to keep the gaff horizontal as it goes aloft. He is in charge of the pace at which the halyard is hauled on. As for the throat halyard, they work as quick as they can to hoist the sail. The mate would keep an eye on the sail as a whole for snags and to make sure it was hoisted in an even and controlled manner. With the kids on board, you need to keep an eye out for reef ties tied together under the boom. Because of the tackle arrangement and the weight difference, the peak would inevitably get ahead of the throat and need to be slowed or even stopped. Very few times have I been able to set sail, main or fore, so that the peak never had to be stopped.

With an eye to where the throat is supposed to ride on the mast and the main boom sits above the saddle, the mate would yell out, "Hold the throat," "Make the throat," and "Go ahead on the peak." The order to hold the throat and make the throat was repeated by the guy at the head of the line. He would put a stopper on the halyard to take the weight off what the passengers were holding, then yell out, "Ready on the throat now. Up behind," meaning the line was to be let go by the passengers and made off by the second crewman on the halyard. "Up behind" is an old term shortened from, "Everyone behind me give up the line." Usually by the middle of the week, the passengers have gotten used to this command and the rope hits the deck with a thundering crack. As this was happening, the mate would keep an eye out for the diagonal wrinkle and stop the peak by saying, "Hold the peak.

Make the peak." This wrinkle should go diagonally between the peak and tack of the sail. This shows the sail is stretched correctly and the peak is at its optimum. As with the throat, the command was repeated by the crew and then the stopper would be put on. Then, as did the throat halyard man, the peak halyard man would yell out, "Ready on the peak. Up behind." Sometimes these commands would be checked by Bob, who would beat the mate to the command or ask for a little bit more or less halyard.

With the mains'l set, one of the crew on each halyard would busy himself with coiling down the halyards. The mate

Ready on the throat.

will yell out, "Stand by your boom lifts. Sing out when you're ready." The second crew that handled the main halyards would go forward to man the fore boom lifts. The mate would wait for the crew to sing out, "Ready on port," or "Ready on starboard." When both were ready, the mate would say, "Slack away together." The fore boom would slowly be lowered down to a position parallel to the water, at which point the mate would yell out, "Hold that. Make that. Stand by your halyards. Sing out when you're ready." The handling of boom lifts is not part of the mains'l setting, because with the main boom, when the sail is down and the boom is in her lifts, there is ample headroom under the main boom. With the fore boom this is not so; hence the extra step. By this time, the two crewmen coiling down the main halyards would be forward, stretching out the fore halyards and instructing the passengers once again to take in hand and space themselves out along the rope. The man at the head of the line would sing out, "Ready on the peak" (or throat). The mate would again sing out, "Haul away together" once both were ready, and the chantyman would start in on another tune, "What do we do with a drunken sailor?"

What will we do with a drunken sailor?
What will we do with a drunken sailor?

Early in the morning
Way hay and up she rises
Way hay and up she rises
Way hay and up she rises

Shave his belly with a rusty razor
Shave his belly with a rusty razor
Shave his belly with a rusty razor

Put him in a long boat till he's sober
Put him in a long boat till he's sober
Put him in a long boat till he's sober

Stick him in a barrel with a hosepipe on him
Stick him in a barrel with a hosepipe on him
Stick him in a barrel with a hosepipe on him

Put him in the bed with the captain's daughter
Put him in the bed with the captain's daughter
Put him in the bed with the captain's daughter

That's what we do with a drunken sailor
That's what we do with a drunken sailor
That's what we do with a drunken sailor

The fores'l hoists in the same way the mains'l did, with the only difference that the mate handles the sheet while keeping an eye for snags, whereas with the mains'l Bob handles the sheet. Once the sail is hoisted to its place, all the same commands used on the main are repeated on the fore. As the halyards are being coiled down, the mate yells out, "Ship your bars," or "Man the windlass."

By this point, about an hour or so has passed since the command was given to "stand by your main halyards." It can take an hour and a half to two hours for *Shenandoah* to be fully underway and coiled down, depending on the swiftness of the crew and conditions of the day. There are a couple of details that I've left out, like bracing the yards to a particular tack in order to reduce windage, but they vary depending on conditions and where we're anchored up. For the sake of this next description, let's say we are anchored in Tarpaulin Cove with a southwest breeze.

With the windlass bars shipped and six passengers, three per bar manning them, the windlass is started and the chantyman starts in on a fresh tune. "Oh, Shenandoah, I long to hear you......"

Fare away, you rollin' river
Oh, Shenandoah, I long to hear you
Away, we're bound away
Across the wide Missouri.

Now the Missouri is a mighty river
Indians camp along her border

Well, a white man loved an Indian maiden
With notions his canoe was laden

Shenandoah, I love your daughter
It was for her I'd cross the water

For seven years I courted Sally
Seven more years I longed to have her

Well, it's fare-thee-well, my dear,
I'm bound to leave you
Fare away, you rollin' river
Shenandoah, I will not deceive you
Away, we're bound away
Across the wide Missouri.

The agonizing process of hauling in the anchor chain begins with that. Unfortunately, after about the third day, volunteers for the windlass become scarce. There are one or two diehards, but it takes coaxing to get manpower. With the windlass going, the crew is placed at different posts around the deck. Two are given the stays'l halyard, two are given the anchor burton, and one is with the bo'sun, manning the stays'l sheet.

Now, in handling the schooner, if the crew knows their jobs—and I mean *all* the crew, mate included—then there is little necessity for the captain to direct the process or get upset while the chain is on its way in. Among professional sailors with an understanding of how to sail or handle a vessel, there should be a certain amount of understanding concerning the process: i.e., seamanship. In our scenario with *Shenandoah* anchored in Tarpaulin Cove, the southwest wind dictates we need to fall off to port.

Tarps is a half moon-shaped cove on the Vineyard Sound side of Naushon Island, Massachusetts. With a southwest wind, as long as it's strong, the schooner rides on her anchor with her aft port quarter to the Sound. If the wind is light, then the schooner can be quite tide-rode. Now any sailor knows that when getting underway from an anchor, it is generally not a good idea to fall off toward the beach. It's a better idea to fall off toward open water. This

means, in our scenario, in order to guarantee *Shenandoah* falls off toward open water, the stays'l has to be sheeted to starboard. This forces the bow to port and starts the schooner out of the cove.

The mate's job during this process is generally to handle the anchor and chain. The bo'sun is in charge of sail handling while keeping an eye on Bob for hand signals. If there is a question about which tack the schooner will fall off on, because we could go either way, you can always find the answer without asking Bob by noticing where he has the main boom tied off. Bob

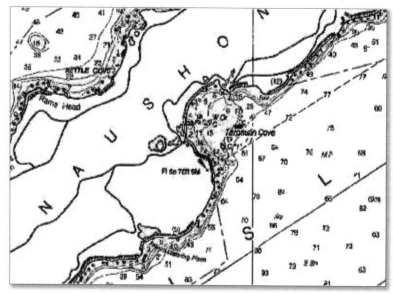

X marks the spot.

always ties the main boom off to one of the yawl boat davits. This forces the stern of the schooner to kick one side or the other. In our Tarpaulin Cove scenario, he would have the boom tied off to port. This kicks the stern to starboard and positions the schooner to take the wind over the starboard rail.

As the windlass bars are worked up and down, the chain comes in over the windlass drum, link by link. The mate concentrates on preventing a "riding turn" while flaking the chain into the chain box. He also keeps an eye on Bob, the wind, crew, and the schooner's place. In my opinion, the anchor chain is probably the mate's greatest foe. He must make sure he does not lose a finger, which has happened, pinched in the chain links while getting a "riding turn."

A "riding turn" is a nightmare, especially if you're close to "short stay," which means the anchor chain is at a very short scope. At this point it would be easy for a gust of wind to break the anchor out of the bottom, inducing the vessel to drag. The "riding turn" would prevent you from paying out more chain and checking the schooner from dragging. Your only choice would be to let go of the port anchor. At this point Bob would be quite upset and may even be on the foredeck. It would also take a month for everything to be right again with you and Bob.

I, thankfully—knock on wood—have yet to get a "riding turn" in or out while dealing with the chain. I have seen them and needed to lend a hand in getting them un-fouled and I've heard some serious stories. It happens when the chain piles up on the inside of the windlass drum. We have all seen it on our jib sheet winches, when the part of the sheet leading from the sail to the winch rides up on the next turn on the drum, locking all the turns together. On the windlass the innermost turn will ride up on the next one and pinch all the chain together. If you see it happening soon enough there is a pinch bar at your feet that you can grab and drive between the chain links to prevent them from riding on each other. Otherwise, if you manage a full riding turn, the only way to relieve the pressure is to rig a four-part tackle onto the anchor chain and down the side deck. This allows you slack at the drum to work the "riding turn" apart.

I always felt that chain out was more stressful than in. You've worked hard to make the schooner go and

Man your bars, boys.

create a comfortable, enjoyable sail for the passengers, and at the end of the day, good sail or bad, you're coming in to the anchorage. Things are happening; the headsails are being taken off, an anchor, weighing in at 600 pounds of iron, is gotten off the rail and lowered down to hang on its chain. The Old Man rounds to where he wants the schooner to sit for the night. She slows, you're watching the water go by the anchor hanging by the chain and you hear the words, "On the bottom" come from aft. So you turn away from the rail and straddle the warping head sticking out from the windlass knee. You put your chest up against the strong back and hang your arms down over the chain on the windlass drum. You need to work slack from the chain box around the windlass and out through the hawse pipe as fast as you can.

At first, the weight of the anchor chain tears the slack you worked around the windlass through the first three turns out of the last turn on the windlass. Then, with the anchor on the bottom, the wind works against the windage aloft and holds the chain under immense pressure; so much so, I have seen four turns ripped off the windlass all at once and there are only four turns there to start with. It just jumps without any warning, no hint, no clue; it just jumps, and always when you're about to grab a chain link.

You work with the pressure of knowing that if you don't get enough chain out, the schooner, 170 tons of wood, iron, and canvas with thirty-five inexperienced passengers aboard, will drag through the mooring field. The chain is heavy at 5 1/3 pounds per foot. Twelve feet make up only what is wrapped around the windlass drum, and it's in such an awkward position that your lower back complains of the weight. Your fingers are on the front line, and the chain is dying for a chance to bite one off. Of course, this has to be done with an air of charisma and nonchalance, because "you never want to let them see you sweat." You get real cozy and close with the chain when you're paying out. Thankfully, you can keep your distance when you're hauling in.

With the chain to "short stay," or as Bob calls it "up short," the staysail is hoisted and sheeted to starboard in this scenario. The windlass becomes very hard because you're breaking the anchor from the suction of hard gray clay on the bottom of Tarpaulin Cove. At this point in getting underway, there is always room for problems; everyone is on edge. The windlass crew crash back and forth and are yelled at by the mate to produce, "Come on, together now," but never seem to get anywhere. The old man is aft watching the oscillation of the schooner for signs of dragging, while the mate is basically helpless but knows what's coming.

The oscillation that Bob looks for from his vantage point is easier to spot from aft than from the mate's position forward. You, as the mate, can still see it in a couple of ways once you have some experience, but it is generally best to let Bob call whether to stop the windlass or proceed. One of the places the mate can see it is in the stays'l. Depending on how tight the sail is sheeted, Bob's call to stop the windlass can come at the same time that a very small luff appears in the sail's luff. The windlass is stopped at this point because the wind is now on the port side of the schooner's center line, when we want the wind on the starboard side of the schooner's center line.

Once the schooner starts back on her oscillation and the stays'l is once again full an' aback, the windlass is started with more vigor. Upon the break, which is fairly easy to see because the windlass frees up, the mate rings the bell, which signals the crew standing by on the outer jib halyard to hoist, as well as letting Bob know we're free of the bottom. Here the bo'sun watches for a signal from Bob on whether to sheet the outer to port or starboard. The sail is never backed unless the schooner is not falling off fast enough. Otherwise the outer jib is sheeted to the tack the schooner is falling off to, to create better steerage and balance for the helm. *Shenandoah* takes, on average, one of her lengths to a length and a half in order to make steerage from a standstill.

While the sail handling is going on, the windlass crew brings the anchor to the surface. With the ring of the anchor breaking the surface of the water, the windlass is stopped, the bars are unshipped, and the anchor burton is called for by the mate. The mate grabs the ring hook and fishes for the ring. On the starboard tack it is imperative to get the anchor catted as quickly as possible. As the schooner falls off and makes way she heels to port, which will swing the anchor to the lee side of the forefoot. If there is any sea on in the process of catting the anchor you can catch a fluke on the forefoot.

This happened to me getting out of Tarpaulin Cove in bad conditions. The whole sail was a nightmare I hope I never have to relive. We were on a week's cruise with adults, before Bob took up chartering the boat with kids. The week had been a hard one weather-wise with lots of wind and rain. We were in Tarps, with clearing conditions, but the wind was still howling. You could see the sea was running big out in the Sound. The passengers could not understand why a big vessel could not handle a big sea. They did not understand that the sea conditions were not conducive for a pleasant afternoon sail. Bob tried to explain why it was best to stay put, but they were very angry and so Bob, against his better judgment, relented.

This started a series of accidents and problems that went on for the whole day. It started with the fluke on the forefoot. The wind was so strong the schooner made speed just about as quickly as she had fallen off on her tack. We were out from behind the lee of the bluff where the lighthouse stands before I got the hook on the ring of the anchor. The sea kept throwing the anchor to leeward of the stem, so I needed a boat hook to slow the flukes down from being thrashed around. It took two or three tries to get the anchor clear of the forefoot. And once catted, the anchor swung so wildly and hard it hit the hull. Bob was yelling about a fluke going through the hull planking and stoving us in. By the time we got the anchor on the rail, we were halfway across Vineyard Sound, going like a freight train.

All of us on the foredeck were soaked to the skin. The outer jib had been struck and the inner had been set. The tacking tackle got pulled out and set up aft on the main boom. After two tries to tack the schooner without success, Bob decided to fall off and wear around. The sea was running so big that once we got our stern to the wind, the sea would grab the yawl boat and pull it away from the stern of the vessel then let it drop against the stern, which made the whole schooner shake.

Once we got the wind to cross the stern and we were on the port tack, it was looking like we might not make it back into Tarpaulin Cove. The sea and the wind had driven us to leeward and we were having trouble pointing high enough to make it back in. Only the crew was on deck at this point. In an attempt to get more power out of the schooner we got the outer jib back on, but no sooner was it set and sheeted in than the clew tore off three feet from the clew iron, bolt rope and everything. The outer jib became a huge flag flogging on the outer jib stay, which shook the entire vessel and sounded like cannons firing. It looked like it was thrashing hard enough to take the fore topmast down.

Myself at the jib.

With Bob yelling about not getting the sail down fast enough, we were working like madmen pulling on the downhaul forward. The wind was so strong it took six of us pulling on that downhaul together to get the sail down. Even with the sail down the wind was so strong the sail continued to flog on the end of the jib boom. The jib boom bounced almost two feet up and down as that sail flogged. I ran out on the jib boom with one of the larger boys in the crew to muzzle the sail and get it tied down. I think it was more work to hang on than to muzzle the sail. No sooner did you notice your stomach in your throat then it was being driven out your…. Well, Bob was still upset back aft and I could not understand what he was saying, though I found out when we got in that night. No sooner did my mate and I get back on the deck when the last of the day's catastrophes occurred: the inner jib sheet let go. Thankfully, this was minor compared with what we had just dealt with. The quick-thinking boatswain held tension on the weather sheet so the sail did not flog. This allowed the crew the ability to reeve a new leeward sheet.

Old King Neptune took pity on us that day and let us get back into Tarpaulin Cove. He must have figured we had learned our lesson. Once on our anchor, we licked our wounds and started in on repairs. The only ones on deck were the crew. Even the poor cook was stuck down below trying to help those who were seasick. Dinner that night in the main saloon was extremely quiet. The wind whistled through the rig outside but the conversation was sparse. The bo'sun, man on watch, and I spent until about two o'clock in the morning putting a new clew and bolt rope on the outer jib, all hand-sewn by kerosene anchor light.

What Bob was trying to get across while we were out on the jib boom was fear of losing men overboard. He did not want us out there on the jib boom for fear of it carrying away, and carrying me away with it. Well, I got a talking to about how if he lost me, the mate, he would have been in a world of hurt. I understood his point but I felt that, as the mate, you're the second-most experienced man on the vessel, the captain being the first, of course, hopefully. It is your job to see that all gets done fast, efficiently, and without casualties. In all the old sea stories, the mate was in the thick of it and once or twice I've read the skipper was too, not safe on the sidelines. Bob swore he knew better, and we got lucky. He said he would never again let people get to him. I think we all, crew and passengers, learned a very important lesson that day.

Catted and fluked, full and by.

So back to our standard perfect takeoff. With the anchor catted and the outer jib set, the mate gets a fluke with the burton. The fluke of the anchor is put on the rail and tied down. As soon as the fluke is on the rail the mate will sing out for the inner jib, if the bo'sun has not beaten him to it. By this point the skipper has had the bo'sun pass the stays'l to leeward. Usually the signal for the stays'l to get passed is having the anchor catted. With the anchor catted, the schooner can make speed without too much trouble being created by the anchor or sea. With the headsails set and the anchor on the rail, the mate will sing out to "coil down," then head aft to find out what the game plan is for the day's sail. The crew coil down and make the halyards into Flemish coils on the deck while the schooner slides along.

"All Home Ready to Hoist"

IN ALL THE SEA STORIES I HAVE SO FAR READ, I HAVE YET TO READ HOW the tops'ls were set or struck. Every year there are many in the crew who are new to the schooner or sailing in general and a description of what goes on is necessary. So I'm going to tell what goes on here and make this book as complete a description of *Shenandoah* and her operation as I can.

Shenandoah has always been a learn-by-doing-it experience, or as Bob likes to say, "on the job training." I think most of the old ships and boats were. Life in general was more like this: At an early age, the young would find themselves in a horse barn, boatyard, or garage just hanging around 'til someone would say, "Hey kid, want something to do?" Lo and behold, you would have an apprentice in the shop. The student or apprentice kept his mouth shut and eyes and ears open to learn the job or trade. It's not a bad way of going about things. I think if one is truly interested in what he or she is involved in, then the person pays close attention and learns every minute detail. If not, they get bored and find something else to be a part of. This process started at a very young age; by the time the person was in their teens, many avenues had been looked into. This does not happen today. The young are sheltered, and then in their late teens or early twenties, it is thrust upon them to figure out what they want to do with their lives. They go to college and learn a whole lot of stuff, but in the end they do something entirely different from their degree. Sorry, I digress.

Yards add a whole different feel and complexity to a vessel. There is more maintenance, more rope, blocks, and more knowledge required to handle the whole mess. With *Pride of Baltimore*, for example, you have the added task of setting the t'gallant from the deck while underway when you want the added sail. *Shenandoah's* t'gallant is a fixed yard, but you do still need a man willing to go aloft and handle some of the gear. I don't feel as though you can judge the financial pros and cons of the squares on many of the small boats, i.e. *Pride* and *Shenandoah*, because these vessels do add a jumping point for those interested in sailing big boats, i.e. *Tovarisch* or *Danmark*. There is also the mystique and romance the topsail schooners give the rest of the fleet around the world.

Turk's head.

As I said in the last chapter, if the conditions are favorable, then, in the process of getting underway, someone would be sent aloft to get the topsails ready to set. We left off in the last chapter with the mate ordering to "coil down" as he went back to see what Bob wanted to do for the day's sail.

We were just out of Tarps with a southwest wind on the quarter as we slid along Naushon Island, bound for Woods Hole. The shore's raw and rough undisturbed beauty, viewed from a nineteenth century vessel, is something I could never describe. This is a most beautiful sight that, in my opinion, is beyond words, or at least my command of them. I would urge you to see it for yourself. In this picturesque place, we have many times set the tops'ls on *Shenandoah*, to the delight of the hopeless romantics.

The command, "Stand by your tops'l gear" would come from aft and be the signal for the crew to get ready to set one or all of *Shenandoah's* three tops'ls. I count her gaff tops'l as one, and will here talk about setting it with the two squares.

"Someone lay aloft on the main," would be the signal for one man in the crew to head up the weather main shrouds and ready the gaff tops'l for setting. I never picked a crewman to head aloft, but let the crew choose among themselves while I ran the deck. I always tried to make it each man's choice. I did require everyone to have a go of it, so that when the day came that there was trouble, I could count on everyone. Sometimes two guys would head up the foremast to handle the topsail and topgallant, but one can do the setting or striking of both sails.

When I started on *Shenandoah*, the stowing of the t'gallant and gaff tops'l were a one-man job and the tops'l was often done by two, but most of the time by four. Actually, the headsails we also did by ourselves, now that I think about it.

Chillin'. *(from the author's collection)*

I used to get all caught up in dealing with the squares while sliding along the southern shore of Naushon Island. It made me think of Edward Teach and his vessel *Queen Anne's Revenge* taking on water in the French watering hole, or the Charles Gray raid, where thirteen English ships of the line sailed the New England coast in 1778. They were held up in Holmes Hole on their way to Nantucket due to weather. Luckily for Nantucket, they escaped a beating, but Martha's Vineyard took it hard. Then there was the Great Republic that spent one tide shift in Vineyard Haven. The thoughts of being aloft, setting squares, still stir feelings in me, but I'll try and stick to the facts.

The men aloft would be getting the gaskets off the sails, which on *Shenandoah* are made of 1/2-inch rope, long enough to spiral around the yard and sail from the outboard end of the yard to the bunt. This gasket is the same port and starboard, as well as on the t'gallant or tops'l. The gasket is untied from the bunt and undone out to the yardarm, where the rope is coiled into a neat fourteen inch-long coil and gasketed. The gasketing is then tied up to the yard, for when the sail is struck and stowed. The crew on deck would get the buntl'ns and leechl'ns off the pins and hold one turn on the clewl'ns. Someone from aloft would sing out, "Ready on the gaff tops'l" or, "Ready on the tops'l," depending on who was ready first. If both were ready, I would set the tops'l before the gaff tops'l so the men aloft the foremast could continue with getting the t'gallant ready for setting while the gaff tops'l was being set.

With the tops'l ready to set, the mate would sing out "Throw 'er off," or "Let 'er go." I used "Throw 'er off." The mate and bo'sun would start in on hauling the tops'l sheets, mate to windward and the bo'sun to leeward. The man aloft would get hold of the jig and let it go, letting the bunt of the sail fly off the yard, while the crew would toss the clewl'ns from the pins and make sure the coils of rope did not tangle as they left the deck. This all goes on at one time and in one motion. Aloft, the man on the yard would then tie the jig up and out of the way of the clewl'n blocks, while keeping an eye for snags and the weather sheet. With the weather sheet, he looks to call it home on the end of the yard. Once the clew of the tops'l is in a place about 8 inches from the check block on the end of the course yard, he will call out, "Starboard home," and "More to port." The bo'sun is usually not too far behind the mate with his sheet of the sail, so most of the time, "Port home" or "Both home, ready to hoist," is heard quite soon after the weather sheet is called.

In this instance, the sail is being set while the schooner is on a starboard tack, which makes the starboard clew the weather one. If we were on a port tack then the port tops'l clew would take precedence in the setting of the tops'l, or t'gallant for that matter. The weather sheet, clew, or leech of the squares'l is always favored while handling the sail for either striking or setting. This keeps the sail under control and prevents it from doing damage to itself or gear. Also the weather clew is where the sail gets its power while in use, so it's fairly important.

With the sheets called and made off on deck, the mate would sing out, "Go ahead on your halyard." Two men in the crew would start pulling as fast as they could and hoist the tops'l yard, stretching the tops'l between its yard and the course yard. Sometimes if Bill was aboard he'd give us a halyard chanty like, "Have you ever been in Rio Grande? Donkey ride'n. Donkey ride'n."

Way hey and a way we go donkey riding donkey riding,
Way hey and away we go riding on a donkey.
Was you ever in Quebec launching timber on the deck,
Where ya break yer bleeding neck riding on a donkey.

Way hey and a way we go donkey riding donkey riding,
Way hey and away we go riding on a donkey.
Was you ever round Cape Horn where the weather's never warm,
Wish to God you'd never been born riding on a donkey.

Way hey and away we go donkey riding donkey riding,
Way hey and away we go riding on a donkey.
Was you ever in Miramichi where they you tie up to a tree,
Have a girl sit on your knee riding on a donkey.

Way hey and a way we go donkey riding donkey riding,
Way hey and away we go riding on a donkey.
Was you ever in Fortune Bay hear the girls all shout hurray,
Here comes Dad with ten months' pay riding on a donkey.
Way hey and a way we go donkey riding donkey riding,
Way hey and away we go riding on a donkey.
Was you ever in Fredericton seeing the king he does come down,
See the king in his golden crown riding on a donkey.

Way hey and a way we go donkey riding donkey riding,
Way hey and away we go riding on a donkey.

The man aloft would step up onto the yard and ride it up while overhauling the gear. Most of the time, Bob calls the yard. "Hold that" would be heard from aft, then repeated by the mate, followed by, "Make that" and "Coil down" from the mate. The mate could, after some time, see where the halyard block comes to rest once the halyard is called. This would allow him to call the halyard before Bob. Remember, this block's placement depends a little on how well the sail is sheeted, as well as whether the sail is wet or dry. Since *Shenandoah* has canvas sails, if they were wet, they would be shrunk up and the halyard block would not be in the same place as if the sail were dry.

The men aloft on the foremast would head up to the t'gallant, and in this rendition the mate sings out, "Stand by your gaff tops'l gear." The man aloft the mainmast at the gaff tops'l would have undone the gasket as well as gotten the bight of tack and sheet off the nut on the spring stay bale before he would yell out he was ready.

The mate, after making sure all was ready, would sing out to "throw 'er off." This would prompt the crew on the halyard to hoist, and the crew on the sheet to haul. The halyard is two-blocked before it's made off and Bob will call the sheet. The tack is pulled 'til either the mate can't take it anymore or someone realizes they've got all they can. The gaff tops'l has always been a light air sail, but the mates have always enjoyed messing with the crew about how the sail is set or trimmed. For some it is too hard to grasp that a piece of cloth is being stretched between three points.

From aloft the foremast we hear "Ready on the gans'l," which is even shorter than saying t'gallant for referring to the topgallant sail.

The mate, bo'sun, and crew take up the same jobs as with the tops'l. The mate sings out to "throw 'er off," and all that happened with the tops'l happens again with the t'gallant. The only difference is the man aloft. With the tops'l, he stands on the yard and rides it up while overhauling the leechl'ns and buntl'ns through the fairleads of the sail. With the t'gallant, he must stand in the shrouds to overhaul this gear for the sail. This is because with the tops'l, the spread of rope is easier to manage on the yard, being that there are six lines to deal with. Two of these lines are more than an arm's length away from you, both port and starboard, at the center of the yard. Overhauling of the gear is important so the sail is not bunched up, but let as free as can be to set well.

On the t'gallant there are only two lines and they are right in your face while standing in the ratl'ns of the fore topm'st shrouds. The only other thing is the t'gallant foot ropes. They hang down on the aft side of the topmast and over the topmast band when the yard is in its lifts, and need to be cleared of this band while the yard is being hoisted. Otherwise, the foot ropes will snag the shackles on the band.

With all the sails set, the men aloft may linger and take in the sights and sounds, but on deck, halyards need flemishing and sheets need coiling. The mate heads back aft to join the afterguard while the crew are left to tidy up.

We would slide along Naushon Island down to Woods Hole. Sheets would be slacked out, yards would be braced around to starboard, and the schooner would roll along without much effort. Down around Woods Hole, we would come up on the wind a little bit. Sheets would be hauled in and the yards braced up sharp so the schooner could build some speed and power to race across Vineyard Sound towards West Chop Light. If a Vineyard ferry was going by, we would trim her well so the schooner made a good picture for the tourists on the ferry. As I have said, my words don't do it justice. It is something you must experience on the deck with the wind blowing by your face and the power of the wooden hull under your feet being driven by the rope and canvas you have just worked.

The power of man.

Striking the squares is not wholly the reverse of setting them. A man aloft is necessary to guarantee no snags and also to call the clews home in the clewl'n blocks. He also calls the leechl'ns and buntl'ns home. He will also call when the yard is in her lifts once the halyard is let go. On deck, the mate would man the halyard and the bo'sun mans the sheets, while the crew hauls on the clewl'ns, buntl'ns and leechl'ns, in that order.

The mate will sing out, "Stand by your gans'l gear." One man would head aloft. The mate would go for the halyard and throw it off, but not just let it fly. It would be a very fast slacking, one that was quick enough so the man going aloft could not make the yard before the yard was in her lifts. When, "yard home," is heard from aloft, the mate would yell out, "Let go your sheets," at which point the bo'sun, who would have the two sheets in hand with one turn around the pins, would toss them from their pins. The mate would yell out to "Clew 'er up," and the crew would pull with everything they had. If it were really windy it might take two to haul on the clewl'ns. Once the clews were home, the mate would ask for the buntl'ns and then the leechl'ns consecutively. The tops'l and t'gallant are the same in their striking, with the exception of buntl'ns. The t'gallant's, buntl'ns, and leechl'ns are one line, but on the tops'l there are four separate buntl'ns and two separate leechl'ns.

The sails would be left to hang in their gear 'til we were on our anchor, then sail was stowed for the night. Once or twice the t'gallant has been struck to shorten sail because the wind has picked up. On these occasions I have gone aloft with someone from the crew and stowed the sail. It can be a bit of a fight, but I've always had fun doing it. I've only stowed the tops'l once while underway, and that was a real fight.

The gaff tops'l does not need a man aloft to strike it. All you need do is lower the halyard so the head of the sail is at the middle band on the topmast. Then let go, tack and sheet, and haul on the ringl'n and clewl'n. This pulls the sail up into a ball just above the main masthead, keeping the sail out of the main peak halyard blocks. On *Shenandoah*, it is not necessary to strike the gaff tops'l when rounding to an anchor or mooring. There is a fair bit of twist in *Shenandoah's* mains'l, so as soon as you start to come on the wind, the gaff tops'l will luff and lose its power. Once or twice I have had a man aloft in the process of stowing the gaff tops'l while the mains'l was being taken in.

"Coil Down"

I T'S ALWAYS BEEN HARD TO GO OUT AND JUST VISIT with Bob on *Shenandoah* and not be a part of her operation. There are always things I see that could use some attention. Of course, Bob is no help either, because he always has a list of things that are bugging him. Sometimes there's someone in the crew interested in learning some little trick or rope work detail. Of course I don't mind that. A number of summers ago I was on the schooner for a week's cruise visiting with Bob. I happened to notice some of the crew was having difficulty with their Flemish coils. They couldn't manage the hackles in the line they were flemishing. In watching them as they worked, it came to me why they were having trouble. In making a Flemish coil there are three steps or, at least, that's how I was taught. The first step is the initial coiling down after the halyard has been used. The second is a tall coil directly from this first coil. Then lastly, the making of the Flemish. The fellows having difficulty with their Flemishes did not do the second part.

Where or how the second step of making a tall coil got lost, I'm not sure. As the crew coils down for the initial long coiling, they leave the coils with the bitter end on the top. This means that if the halyard ever needs to be struck quickly, someone would have to have the forethought to flip the coil so that it will run free without snags.

There have been many times when something must get struck quickly after it's just been set. Once or twice after being in this predicament, I had seen it coming, and so ordered a Ballantyne coil made. This is a coil done on the deck with the diameter of about 30 inches or more, depending on the length of the rope, and a three leaf clover design to it. Again, the halyard is long coiled, starting at the belaying pin, and worked to the bitter end. Once at the bitter end, instead of flipping the coil over, you make a circle with three turns, about 30 to 36 inches in diameter. Then you start with a smaller loop going in towards the center and then out towards the outer perimeter. Another small loop goes in towards the center and then back out towards the outer perimeter. Finally the third small loop is placed in towards the center and worked out toward the outer perimeter. This gives you your three leaf clover appearance. You continue this process until you run out of rope, which will bring you back to the belaying pin. This Ballantyne coil is flimsy and can be knocked over and tangled easily, but it's very fast to produce and an excellent way to get a piece of rope to run fast without any snags.

Manila rope is in constant movement, basically because it's wood. It shrinks and swells depending on the humidity of the day. It also has a great bit of stretch, and while being worked in the rig and through tackle it builds up tension. The rope is under load, and then slack. In the process of long coiling, you slowly work any tension or twist to the free end of the rope. With the tall coil you take that rope and turn it into a tight circle, but also work tension out to the free end of the rope for a second time. This is done because both times you start at the belaying pin and work towards the bitter end. Without coiling the rope down, once long and then tall, you will get kinks in the rope while trying to make the finished Flemish. While dealing with new rope I have had to long coil a line as many as four times before the rope would be free enough of hackles to Flemish.

The first coiling down of the halyard is done by the man who belayed the halyard. The coil is done on the deck in a long coil way. This means it's large and oval-shaped. It's worked from the belaying pin to the end of the rope. Once at the end of the rope, the entire coil is picked up and flipped over. This puts the bitter end on the deck and the bottom of the coil and the belaying pin on the top of the coil. This is done so that, if it is at all necessary, the halyard can be let go quickly without the coil snagging as it runs free.

Ship shape.

Once the schooner is underway and the command is given to "coil down," the crew goes back to the halyards and continues with step two in the process of Flemishing. The second step is to make a tall coil from the long coil lying on the deck. They start from the belaying pin again and make the coil small, but on top of itself. With the peak and the throat halyards, we used to make tall coils 20 to 24 inches in diameter and sometimes as tall as the rail is high (at about your waist). I was shown a great picture of Brooke, Bob's youngest son, in a tall coil years ago. The coil was quite big—ah no, Brooke was quite small!

With this tall coil done, the bitter end is now on the top of the coil. With the bitter end, you start the Flemish. The Flemish coil is three stacks of rope with the bitter end on the bottommost stack. The rope should come out of the center of the finished coil on the top stack and go straight to the belaying pin without any extra. This takes a little time to figure out because each halyard is different. I seem to remember the stays'l halyard coil was six deck planks wide. The main throat and peak were easy because they were as big as the space between the cabin house and the waist. One of the Flemish coils as I remember was eight planks wide and I think it was the outer jib but that doesn't help us do the Flemish.

With the tall coil done and the bitter end in hand, one can now start to make the base for a Flemish. Let's say we're working on the stays'l halyard. Make a large loop six planks in diameter and work the line towards the center of this diameter. Keep each turn snug up against the last, but only side by side. Once in the center, go back out to the outermost edge to create the second level, and again work your way around towards the center. Once there, again go back out to the outermost extreme and work your way back again towards the center of the third level. Remember to make the second pass of "center to outer extreme" opposite that of the previous level's pass. If you make the passes of "center to outer extreme" on top of each other, then the Flemish will be poorly shaped. If all went well, you should come right out of the center of the Flemish and lead up to the belaying pin without extra rope.

These Flemishes are very durable on the deck. You can walk on them, and they will withstand the deck being flooded with sea water as the schooner is heeled over. Like a Ballantyne coil, the halyard will run quite freely when asked. They are much easier to handle than coils of rope hung on the pin rail or sheer pole, and they look very sharp strewn about the deck. On those long tacks, the bigger Flemishes make great pillows for a nap on the warm, sunny deck.

Gaff Tops'l

IN PUTTING THIS BOOK TOGETHER, I TRIED TO ADD a good sea story or two in all the chapters so that the reading isn't entirely boring details. Unfortunately, I don't have a good war story about *Shenandoah's* gaff tops'l to put in this chapter. So I've chosen one from a different page of my life aboard *Ampelisca*, a little English cutter my folks have owned since 1977 and sailed up and down the eastern coast. The old gaff tops'l, or as the English call it, jib-headed tops'l, really lives a simple life. It's a straightforward sail with few lines that I have never minded dealing with. *Shenandoah's* is fairly large, having a 50-foot luff and 25 to 30-foot miter. *Shenandoah's* topmasts are rigged with a backstay halfway up the mast. Her gaff tops'l is loose on the luff above this lower topmast backstay, and has five mast hoops holding the sail to the mast below this backstay. The sail has been put up in the beginning of the season as a tight little bundle, and sometimes as a huge flag.

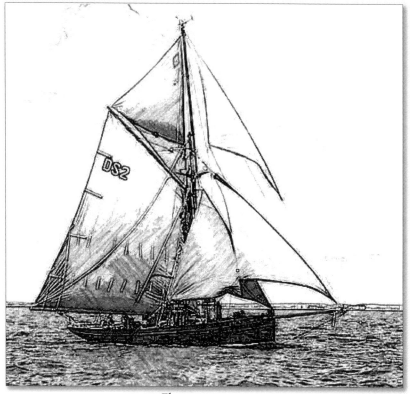

Elegance in motion.

I've always gone about working on *Shenandoah* with a lay-low, keep-quiet approach. The vessel is big enough and under enough scrutiny that there is no reason to add to it. I figured with this approach, when the day comes that something goes wrong, fewer people will notice. I have no problem admitting the learning curve was painful once or twice over the years, but thankfully, my mistakes went mostly unnoticed and without any casualties. Of course this approach has had fallout, too. The tasks assigned me have gotten bigger and harder to accomplish.

Anyway, as you may have guessed, I prefer the tight bundle approach. It's neat, clean, and can be done in a gale of wind by only one person. The key to success with this sail, or anything for that matter, is the prep. I would stretch the sail out on the after deckhouse with the luff on the centerline of the vessel and the clew on the side deck. The head will be back by the wheel and the tack by the cook's doghouse. With the sail laid out like this, the sail's port side would be on deck and the starboard side would be facing the sky. I would reeve the ringl'n and clewl'n through the sail and coil them at the head. Once the sail is up and bent, these lines can be rove through the lubber hole and dropped to the deck. The ringl'n leads from the head of the sail down the center through fairleads to the tack, while the clewl'n runs from the head of the sail along the leech to the clew through a fairlead and then along the miter to the nock. These two lines cross in the middle of the sail, but it does not matter which one is under the other. I've done it both ways and cannot say there is a noticeable difference.

With the gear rove off in the sail, you now can flake it down into a tight bundle. I have tried to furl the sail as it is furled on the mast, but that's a little difficult. So the easiest thing I've found to do is take the upper section, meaning the length of bolt rope between head and topmost mast hoop eyelet, on the luff and fold it in half, so that the head is at the first mast hoop eyelet and there's a bight of cloth looped down towards the tack. Now do the same thing with the tack, folding it in the center, but with the tack at the nock and the bight of bolt rope up toward the head. This should leave a section of bolt rope from nock to topmost mast hoop eyelet exposed. Now you can flake the sail down against the luff where the mast hoops will seize on. If you start your flaking at the bolt rope, you will end with the clew on the top of the flakes. This is a good thing because you need to tie the sheet on once the sail is aloft. If you want to get fancy, leave the very first flake larger than the rest so you can use it as a skin to roll around everything that you flake down. All the parts can still be exposed but the skin puts the finishing touch on the bundle. Gasket this up nice and tight then use the gaff tops'l halyard to hoist the sail aloft.

Aloft, this sausage should hang just below the lower topmast backstay iron. With the sail hanging here, you can hank the mast hoops in place with ease. There can be no confusion with lashing the hoops to the luff in the wrong orientation. The sail cannot be twisted or have incorrect bends in the bolt rope for the sail to set properly. Once the mast hoops are hanked on and the "GT" sheet is tied to the clew, the gaskets can be cut one by one so the sail can fall to be furled.

From the full-rigged ship down to the catboat, the traditionally-rigged vessel is a very diverse group of sailing ships. With my parents in the wooden boat building and restoration business, as well as knowing Bob and his friends, I've been very lucky over the years with the opportunity to sail many different types of these vessels. One time on *Ampelisca*, we set her jib headed tops'l above a main that had two reefs in. From another vessel, she probably looked a very different sight, but the sail combination was really quite good.

We were visiting with George Cadwalader at his place in Woods Hole. He had a house on a barge there in Great Harbor, and we were rafted up to it while on a short fall cruise in October. On this day, we got underway at about ten in the morning. We had a real strong northeasterly with a good sea running, but Christian and I had school on Monday, so we had to head out. After pushing out into Buzzards Bay, we got the main and stays'l on the old girl. *Ampelisca*, with her English pilot cutter heritage and eighteen tons of displacement, handled the sea well, but it became necessary to roll in two reefs. We also needed to set her spitfire jib to make her a bit easier to steer. We rode the day out like this 'til we got down by Cuttyhunk Island, at which time the wind started to have holes in it. It would gust up hard, then die out, and when it was light the sea would wreak havoc by tossing *Ampelisca* around. The sea was running about six feet at the base of Buzzards

Good sea rising.

Bay, and in the lulls she would roll and the gaff would thrash, jarring the rig. Letting out a reef was not going to be good for when the wind piped up again, but our speed was dropping, so we tried the tops'l.

One drawback of a gaff-rigged sail is the gaff. It's heavy, and in light air will swing out of control. Also, with a gaff sail there is a lot of roach and a small amount of luff. Compared to a Bermuda rig, luff roach proportions are reversed. Roach is great off the wind, but luff is the power behind the aerodynamics of a sail. By setting the gaff tops'l, we add luff length without that much roach. On *Ampelisca* the tops'l sets "on the fly," meaning without hanks or a lace line attaching it to a mast or stay. This made it possible to fly the sail sheeted off the gaff where it should fly normally set. The head of the sail flew by the lower masthead instead of at the topmast head.

Well, we ran this way up to Dutch Harbor in Narragansett Bay. It was a great sail. We were able to keep the speed up and the gaff under control. *Ampelisca* can turn her heels up if she is handled well and she proved it that day when we got into Dutch Harbor at five. The only trouble we had was Dad did manage to make it back into port and my brother and I did make the bus; we were hoping for an extra day off.

So with *Shenny's* sail hanging down, the mast hoops all fall towards the masthead on the top of the cap iron. The halyard needs to be lowered to the same place. The tack is the first part of the sail that you make fast to the cap iron. Make a bight out of the line of the tack and loop it over the bolt at the cap iron. The next thing I would do is take the bight of cloth made between the tack and nock to the masthead and tie with a hitch made with the tack line just under the cap iron. Once that is secured, you can bring the clew up to the iron. The sheet can be made into a bight and looped under the horseshoe band and hooked on the bolt of the cap iron, the same as the tack.

With all this canvas hanging down from the iron, you slowly flake it and pull it down, laying it against the mast little bits at a time. Start from the inside and work your way out. The skin is created by the miter, starting at the nock. With the sail pulled down and laid against the mast, the skin is stretched over the whole mess and made into a tight sausage. At the iron, to get the sail to lie nicely, the bights of bolt rope between the mast hoops are pulled out and rolled down under the skin. Starting at the masthead, you can use the gasket and work your way down the sail, making it tight as you go along. At the crosstrees there is an excess of cloth that needs to be "bear hugged" in order to get it crushed down.

Now this is the basic furl of the gaff tops'l on *Shenandoah* that Robbie, one of Bob's sons, showed me. As with all things, there are many small details and tricks too hard to express in words for me, but that make for a tight and smooth stow. Those finer points I'm going to leave for you to figure out. Good luck, and enjoy the view from aloft while stowing.

The Wharf Rats

THE ANCHOR BURTON ON *SHENANDOAH* is an odd tackle arrangement for lifting the anchors. It is powerful, lightweight, and compact. It can be used wherever you need to get a heavy job done. Alternatively, there's the throat halyard. The throat halyard with its jig is more powerful, but it can be a bear to "fleet out" or stretch when you want it long, whereas the burton is easy. This makes the burton a perfect choice for repetitive tasks like getting the cannon or sails in and out of a skiff in the spring or fall.

The burton, or fish tackle to the Downeasters, is very simple, nothing more than an upside down Spanish Burton with a slight modification. The single is on deck, instead of aloft or overhead as is typical. Having a single to handle up at the cathead or by the fluke is much less work than a double, which is the norm. Also, in *Shenandoah's* burton, there's a four-part tackle in the mix of blocks. This gives an eight-to-one advantage instead of the typical half-to-one. The single, being on the bottom, is rigged to advantage, which cuts the weight by half. Okay, so it's a little more than a slight modification. The burton is rove like so, a standard four-part tackle with the hauling end led off the top block of the two doubles. The working block or lower block of the four-part tackle has a line shackled to its becket. This whip is rove through a single and then back through a fairlead iron on the lower double and up to the hauling block or top block shackled under the course yard. The bitter end is seized to the becket on the top of the top block.

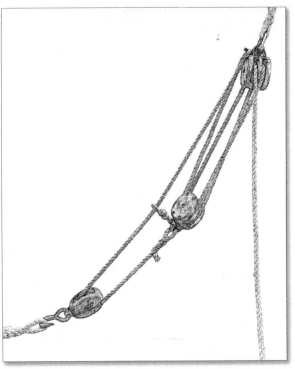

Burton.

One time I moved a topmast with the anchor burton from one side of the schooner to the other. Cannon and sails are a standard job in the spring or fall for fit out or tear down. There is no need for a backache when the burton is hanging around watching what's going on.

I grabbed my motorcycle off the dock at Kelly's Shipyard in Fairhaven with the anchor burton.

We had finished our haul out and were back in the water alongside the dock waiting for Charlie with his tugboat, *Jaguar*, to take us in tow back to the Vineyard. So I didn't have to pay the ferry cost and run the bike down to Woods Hole, I put the bike on the deck of the schooner. When we were back in Vineyard Haven, I moved it onto the paint barge and took it ashore, where I rolled it up the beach.

The anchor burton makes me think of the anchors. Yes, I know the anchors have nothing to do with rigging, but on *Shenandoah* they are a very important bit of gear, because *Shenandoah* has no button to push that gives you a gentle vibration in the deck, nor a lever to engage a propeller giving you firmness of position, and of course no throttle to push down on which makes that bearing on the beach that you've been eyeing for the last half hour go from sliding forward to inching aft. Without internal power, no engine, nothing to fall back on when you find you've made the wrong choice about your holding ground or your position when the wind shifts, there's no second chance. You need to do it right the first time on *Shenandoah*. I've seen the port anchor put to use twice: once in Cuttyhunk and once in Nantucket. Actually, now that I think of it, the most chain I've seen out was three quarters of a box, which is about 200 feet, and I've seen four turns jump off the windlass drum when she snubs her chain. Usually one more flake will take care of this, but sometimes it takes two.

Straining at the bits.

In Vineyard Haven on the mooring where one more flake is not an option, due to there not being room behind us to fall back in, we would take a turn around the warping head. This would put teeth marks in the windlass bits and you would feel the schooner shiver after every wave that hit her forward flare while trying to drive her ashore. Once I remember thinking we were going to tear the windlass out of the deck. The northeast wind was so strong and the sea was running in the head of the harbor so hard that the tops of the waves would flood in the scuppers. She would be hit in the bow so hard that green water would force its way through the hawsepipes and would shoot over head going for the foremast while we were standing alongside the fo'c'sle 'atch. This puts a certain feeling in the air about one's surroundings, one I don't believe you can grasp unless you've either been on the deck of a vessel, or you're her owner sitting in your truck at Packers Wharf watching your baby straining to hold on.

The time in Nantucket when the port anchor was asked to lend a hand was not an ideal execution, though I'm not sure you can have an ideal execution when all hell breaks loose. I guess, as the passengers claimed, we had the Lord looking over us, or maybe we just got lucky. It had been a great day of wandering around town, popping into antique shops, one in particular that Bob was fond of. He said, "I always find something I can't live without in this place." I came out with a wooden barrel spyglass.

We had ice cream and a visit to the Wharf Rat Club to meet up with Charlie. That's Charlie Sayle, Zeb Tilton's mate! What a day to meet Charlie Sayle in the Wharf Rat Club. The clubhouse was filled with artifacts and pictures of members holding the club burgee at different places around the world. The place was a little one-room shack down on the water with a big center table and chairs all around. I seem to remember a little woodstove in the corner or at one end of the room. There were so many pictures and artifacts to take in and I was trying to pay attention to what Bob and Charlie where talking about. I can't remember all the details.

I also can't remember if it was this day or another time we visited Nantucket when Charlie took us up to his house to have tea with the missus and wander around his little shop. I remember Bob and him talking about the name boards Charlie was making for *Alabama*, which he had on his bench. "Yeah, Bob I'll finish them when you get the boat rigged up," said Charlie. That little shop was full of amazing stuff, much like Bob's shop on the Vineyard and my parents' shop in Wickford. I guess great minds think alike. I've been lucky over the years and have met some cool people, I think.

After our outing was over, we found our way back to the schooner, had our dinner, listened to Billy's music, and went to bed. We had originally got in to the anchorage and anchored with a southwest wind, but during the day the breeze boxed the compass and settled down in the northwest. Of course, in Nantucket it made no difference because the harbor is a giant swimming pool; no high land but a good breakwater. With the breeze veering and the tide going in and out during the course of the day, our starboard anchor had fouled, so that at about midnight when I was wishing the crew on watch a good night, I noticed we were closer to the mooring field than we had been all day. The breeze piped up fairly good and apparently had dragged us to the edge of the mooring field.

While getting the old man up to put the yawl boat under the stern to try and reset the anchor, we got into the mooring field. Bob went running down the deck for the port anchor. He pried it off the rail and started paying out chain. While he and I paid out chain on the two anchors, the passengers, a religious youth group from North Carolina, were in the main saloon praying and singing hymns. The crew was trying to get the boats on the moorings off the sides of the schooner.

Then, out of the darkness coming up the channel, was Ralph Packer's tug *Thuban*, with an oil barge in tow. Bob ran back to the aft cabin and got on the horn to *Thuban* to ask about giving us a yank out of the mooring field. After *Thuban* dropped the oil barge at the dock, she came right over, tossed us a line and took a strain, which put a stop to our draggin' ashore. Boy, was it nice having the smell of diesel out in front on the other end of that line.

To the rescue.

As *Thuban* pulled us ahead, we took in our anchors. What a mess! The port anchor was in the starboard anchor's chain and the starboard anchor had a full hitch around one fluke. It took us a couple of hours, almost till morning, to get those two anchors cleared of each other. We had tackle rigged on the bowsprit and tackle rigged on the cat head. We even had the yawl boat up under one anchor trying to get those anchors and chain all untangled. Once we got it all cleared, we got the starboard anchor back on the bottom. *Thuban* went back to her oil barge and we went back to bed.

Next day David, the troop leader, was pretty happy. He figured the hymns and prayers had made all the difference. The rest of that week was full of discussion regarding the great powers that be. There may be some truth in what he said, but that's not for me to decide.

In Cuttyhunk the port anchor was far more effectively employed, and it was a damn good thing, since the spot we were in was tight. We had just gotten through Quick's Hole when the wind gave in, so over went the yawl boat to push up into Cuttyhunk's outer harbor. The horizon to the west was dark, but the forecast was for southwest. The closer we got to Cuttyhunk, the darker the horizon got, but when we got in off the bell, the anchor went down. The crew had just come down from stowing the square sails when it hit. It really did look as if it was going to stay on the mainland, but no. We got a gust on the beam from the northeast so hard that the old schooner rolled to her side and put her scuppers in the water. We had six inches of water standing in the waterway. She stood there for a second, maybe longer, but in that second or two the heavens opened up and the rain came down like a waterfall. It was so solid that it was like twilight. The schooner pulled four turns off the windlass as she strained and turned to the wind. As she came to, she righted herself and came up right.

Shenandoah is very steady on her anchor or mooring. She weathervanes nicely and doesn't sail on her chain like many vessels do. This also makes it very easy in an anchorage to get on or off an anchor. Speaking of anchors, Bob had got the port anchor off the rail and while we paid out chain, four turns were ripped off the windlass every time we took a break. By the time we had half a box out to starboard and five flakes to port, the squall passed. The sun came out, the wind died, and the rain stopped. It was back to what it was like when we had gone through the hole: flat calm, bright, and heavenly. In the rush of the event, the main flag halyard had gotten away from someone while swapping out the good flags for storm flags. Bob got a little upset about that, he was stressed given what just happened. All in all, it was a great exercise in keeping one's head and working to protect the vessel and her cargo. "Cargo is king." (Irving Johnson)

Every three years ...

THE BLOCKS ARE NOT SOMETHING I have been interested in writing about. To write down what I see in all the different blocks is a little daunting in my mind because each block has little clues as to its place in the rig. It is true I have become so familiar with them that I can pick out any block from a pile on *Shenandoah's* deck and tell you for what and where it is used. I've never had trouble with the blocks and rigging of boats or vessels; all of their aspects have come easily for me. Living aboard boats, in and around boatyards, and working on boats for my entire life has had an impact, I guess.

Every three years, all the blocks on *Shenandoah* are taken in to the shop and broken down into their various parts. They are repainted, re-greased, and then put back together. Who does this overhaul job dictates how much grief I have in the spring. Once or twice it's happened that the blocks have been put back together so they all look nice and are symmetrical on the bench but wrong for the rig. For example, something simple

The block.

like the lower yard braces, which shackle onto the twelfth ratline from the rail, port and starboard on the main shrouds. On the port side the keeper is outboard and the shackle pin goes in from the top down, but on the starboard side the keeper is also outboard and the pin goes from the top down. On the bench, the keepers of these two blocks should face you with the shackle pins opposing each other, not so they both go in from left to right.

I realize this may seem like no big deal for many reasons. I'm too picky, too anal; just swap the shackles and problem solved. Yes, this is true, but to swap shackles means taking the blocks apart because the shackles are captured in place by the becket. To have the shackles correct is important to the safety of the vessel. The keepers, which are diamond shaped copper covers over the block's sheave pin, are for looks alone, but if you keep track of the little details, then the finished product will be a grand sight.

Thankfully the dreaded disassembly of the blocks only happens every three years and only affects the poor crew tasked with putting them all back together. The crew who took them apart always give the blocks silly names and put silly pictures on the tags, making it difficult to figure out which block is which if you're not familiar with the rig.

The blocks are no great mystery unless you can't see the function or don't understand the rule of thumb on *Shenandoah*. This is basic and may seem trivial but it does aid in the placement of many blocks about the rig. The rule goes like this: "All the diamonds or keepers that can, face the starboard side." This is the side of the vessel that all the passengers board and only pertains to blocks that do not have a symmetrical partner. "All the shackle pins that can go in from the top down." This ensures that the pins never fall out if they come unscrewed. Many vessels mouse the shackle pins, which is fine. On *Shenandoah* that has never been done, and in all my years I've yet to see a pin unscrew from its shackle on any vessel I have sailed.

This covers many of the blocks on *Shenandoah*, but there are, as with all things in life, exceptions. So the exception is, "All of the blocks to handle the topsail gear have their keepers face forward or face port and starboard. Their shackles do the same thing; the pins either go in from forward or, in the case of symmetrical placement, in from port or starboard." With the shackles, the ones that go in from forward still go in on a

Simplicity.

downward slant, since the masts on *Shenandoah* are so raked, but the pins that go in from port or starboard are done for symmetrical reasons. If we were to look at the topsail sheets for an example, the fairlead blocks under the course yard have the sheaves athwart the vessel, which puts the diamonds facing forward and the shackles in from port and starboard.

If we look at the outer jib, which is an exception, the keepers are facing port. This is because of how the tackle is rove, where the halyard is belayed and is shackled on the mast. The outer downhaul is

on the port side of the jib boom, and this means the head of the sail is stowed to port. With this understanding, we know the keeper of the downhaul block will face port, so that its backside is against the stowed sail. Also with the halyard, because the masthead block is shackled onto the port side of the mast band, the backside of the block will lie against the mast and the keeper will face port. With the way the becket is in the blocks, the shackle pins have to go in from forward, on both the upper end of the jib halyard and the downhaul block. The block that's attached to the head of the sail will then be rove so that its keeper faces port. The shackles of these blocks are actually kind of screwy, because none of them fit the heads of the sails well, but the pins should still go in from the top down. With the jib halyards—outer jib, inner jib, and staysail—the blocks are all for ¾-inch line. The hauling part of the outer jib halyard leads aft of everything and inboard of the spreaders. Then it gets made on the aftmost belaying pin of the port fore pin rail.

The inner jib is the opposite of the outer jib, since the downhaul is on the starboard side. So for show, the keeper faces starboard, and the backside is against the furled sail. Also, the halyard is set up so the keepers are to starboard and all the shackles are forward to aft. The hauling end of this halyard is also led aft of everything, inside of the spreaders but down to the aftmost pin on the starboard fore pin rail. All the blocks that are used for the jib heads are heavily grooved from wearing on the wire stays.

Bowsprit.

With the stays'l, I stow the head of the sail to starboard, which means putting the keeper of the block on the head facing the starboard side. At the trestle trees, the block is keeper forward. This is because the stays'l halyard shackles to an eyebolt on the starboard trestle tree of the foremast. The eyebolts that were used to take the halyard for the lower yard are positioned fore and aft, and with the stays'l halyard shackled to it, the block rests athwartships. The masthead block is on the port trestle tree eyebolt with a fairlead block in the shrouds to jump the halyard over the lower yard. The hauling end then goes down to the second pin from forward on the port fore pin rail. Consequently, the second pin from forward on the starboard pin rail is for the anchor burton and the first belaying pin on both sides is the stays'l sheets.

Many of the blocks have telltale characteristics that give a hint to their particular tasks in the rig; it's almost not worth labeling them. All of the twenty-three 1-inch blocks for the main and fores'l are easy to spot. The mainsheet blocks and foresheet blocks, for starters, can't be confused with the throat and peak halyard blocks because the triples have sister hooks on them and the doubles are leathered, one of which has a becket. This one is for the fore sheet, and the other one is for the main. The triples and the doubles for the throats do not have shackles, either. And, if you look closely, you will notice the triples are worn heavily on two cheeks of two sheaves on opposite sides. There is a single leathered with a swivel for the foresheet, and there are two singles, oiled and carved, for the mainsheet.

Dan Moreland gave the carved blocks to Bob shortly after one of his round the world trips on the *Picton Castle*. The triple block with the rounded shoulders on the shell for the main sheet is off the *Morrissey*.

There are four singles with hooks that are used for the fairlead blocks on the main and fore peak and throat halyards which hook onto eyebolts in the deck. This leaves six singles and two doubles which are all for the peaks, main and fore. Two singles per gaff with a single and a double per masthead.

So now the pile is not so big. Simple, right? There are only two 3/4-inch triple blocks on the whole boat, and they are used for the yawl boat falls. Also, there are only two 3/4-inch doubles with hooks, again used for the yawl boat falls. These blocks are impressive because their spacers between the cheeks, the swallows, are bronze. The triples were acquired from Sam Norton, who was the skipper of *Manxman*, a 130-foot cutter. He had a junkyard of sorts, full of military leftovers. The port anchor also came from him. Bob told me that Sam could make *Manxman* fetch up Edgartown Harbor round the point by the Chappy ferry and with her momentum range up the whole inner anchorage.

The topsail halyard is made up out of two double ¾-inch blocks, which makes it a four-part tackle. One block is nondescript, but the other has a metal strap with chain attached to the top becket and is to guide the block along the topmast backstay when in service. There are two such blocks, actually; the second and smaller is the t'gallant halyard. It also has a nondescript counterpart, which makes it a four-part tackle as well. Two very distinctive blocks used in the tops'l and t'gallant halyards are very old, oiled, and very round in shape. One has a long chain on it; the other has a wire, although they both had chain when I started on the schooner. As you may figure, the small one is for the t'gallant and the other the tops'l. The tops'l block was once a whip block on the *Jane Dora*, *La Dona* before that, which Bob owned at one time. She is up in Maine now, as the *Nathaniel Bowditch*.

In this pile of blocks you will see six half-inch doubles with hooks. They are all for the small boat falls and have six corresponding doubles with beckets. They are the only ones of their kind, and so the pile gets smaller. So 1/2-inch blocks, two singles with about a foot of 3/4-inch chain on them, are used for the t'gallant leechl'n blocks. There are also two doubles with about a foot of 3/4-inch chain and they're for the tops'l buntl'ns.

Two of the three blocks for the anchor fall are easy to spot because one is a 3/4 inch single with a hook. The other is a 3/4 inch double with a steel bracket that has an eye in the end of it, but the second double is nondescript. The iron eye is a guide for the single part of the burton setup.

There are seven little odd blocks that are big enough to receive a 3/4 inch shackle in their becket and sheaves for a 1-inch line, but the blocks are only 2 inches in diameter. Four of these are used as fairlead blocks on the four and main throat halyards and one on the stays'l halyard. The other two are used for the peak and throat halyard blocks of the fisherman.

There is only one more block that has an obvious appearance to it and that is the gaff topsail sheet block. It's the only one with a wire strop on it and it slips over the end of the main gaff. This is one of two blocks for this sheet. The other has nothing special about it, but shackles under the gaff jaw to port.

This accounts for all of the blocks that have details that set them apart from all the rest. What you're left with is about twenty doubles with and without beckets for 3/4 inch and 5/8 inch line. There should also be about thirty-three singles that are also with and without beckets. Three-quarter, 5/8, and ½-inch line should fit through them. All the doubles are for the main and fore jigs and boom lifts. The singles make up the braces, lower lifts, tops'l and t'gallant sheets, jib down hauls, gaff tops'l sheet and halyard, and tops'l and t'gallant clewl'n and leechl'n.

This last pile of blocks may sound like a lot and/or a copout on my part in not describing each in detail, but there is no real ID-ing these blocks for specific places. The jigs are all 5/8 inch, four-part tackle, and the lifts are 3/4 inch four-part tackle. The braces and lower lifts are gun tackles made with ¾-inch blocks, except for the t'gallant which is a single part brace but still three-quarter line. So see, it's not too hard to figure out the rest of the gear. If you're reading this to rig *Shenandoah*, well, you need to use your own brain a little.

Hard Row

SHENANDOAH HAS THREE SMALL BOATS ON DAVITS, four if you include the yawl boat. But for the moment, we will just look at the two Whitehalls and the Bahamian dinghy. The Whitehalls were built by Dick Shoew and are written up in *Building Classic Small Craft* by John Gardner. As for the Bahamian dinghy, she was built by William Alberry and Bob acquired her in Miami while he was putting time in with the Air Force back in '56. He bought her to sail the inland waterway during his off time.

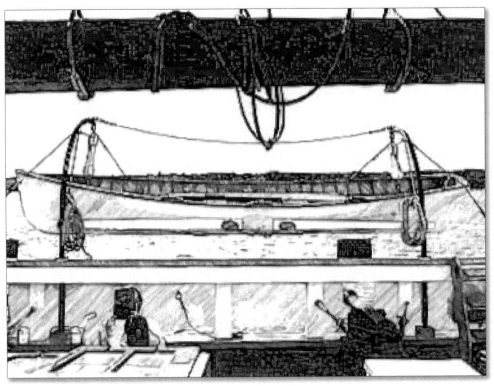

Starboard boat.

All three boats' falls are rigged similarly, their keepers face forward and aft and the hooks for the lower blocks of the tackle all face forward or are open forward. The hauling parts are reeved so that they are led from the inside sheave of the top block. While standing on deck facing the boat hanging in its davits you can see these aspects. For example, the port Whitehall's bow is to your right when you face the boat. All the hooks are open to your right as you face the boat. The stern fall's keepers are to your left and the hauling part is reeved over the right sheave of the top block. The bow fall's keepers are to the right and the hauling part is reeved over the left sheave of the top block. With the hauling parts reeved in this way, the starting point of this tackle needs to be on the top block, so the top block has the becket on it. The becket is to your left for the stern fall and your right for the bow fall. This is the same for the Bahamian dinghy, but not so for the starboard Whitehall. The starboard Whitehall is a mirror image of the port side boat's falls. This difference only matters with regards to the blocks and how they are put together, if it's a block year. The top blocks on this Whitehall's falls have the shackles opposite that of the port Whitehall and Bahamian dinghy. All else is the same. The shackles for the top blocks are put together so that the pins go from inboard to outboard. This makes it easy to hook the gear up and tighten down the shackles. These falls are rigged up in this manner for a couple of reasons. With the hauling parts rigged to the inside, their leads correspond with hooks and cleats welded to the inside of the davits. The Bahamian dinghy's davits have no hooks welded to the inside of the davit but the falls are still rove in this manner. This makes for no twists in the top block that would otherwise chafe the cheek or excessively wear on the fall.

The hooks all face forward in case one of the boats needs to be launched while the schooner is underway. This may not be apparent unless you're in the boat hooking or unhooking a fall, as the boat is being dragged through the water by the schooner moving ahead. It is much safer with the hooks in this attitude, for they fall onto or off their eyes in the boat. The stern fall is always let go first and hooked up second. Then you unhook the bow fall and the drag of the boat is put against the painter, which should be manned before the boat is lowered into the water. This is done to keep the bow of the boat from being swamped by waves coming down the side of the schooner. The man on the bow fall should be good at "fishing" a hook and keeping the nose of the boat up.

Rowing into an angry sea – "a roller coaster ride." (image by Dan Urish)

One time during a northeast gale, we got so bored hanging out aboard the schooner that we decided to go for a row in a Whitehall boat. The sea was licking the scuppers in Vineyard Haven Harbor and we had been sitting there for two days. We had passengers on and everybody was getting a little antsy. The crew was looking for an escape from the passengers and the passengers were looking for some action. We were looking for some action. We were having a hard time getting people off the schooner to go ashore with the sea running the way it was.

So, like I said, some of us in the crew decided to jump in a Whitehall boat and go for a row. Now I can't say this was a smart idea; I'd never do it now nor let the crew do it, but at the time we figured it was no big deal and we could handle it. It's not very often that young people do things very smart. Getting that boat in the water was a blunder. Fishing the hooks was a failure and one of the falls hooked a seat and tore it out. The boat beat against *Shenandoah's* topsides and probably broke some frames. Three of us tumbled into that boat and pushed off, heading for the breakwater. It was a good thing three of us went because we definitely needed two on the oars and one to bail. Each wave rolled over the stem, and for one or two it was more than just the top of the wave. But we were pumped, on a mission, though the mission wasn't really anything. After a while it got tiring and we realized that bringing the boat about was going to be tricky.

I don't remember how we got the boat about but we managed it. We didn't upset her, I remember that. We might have made it to the breakwater by the drawbridge and turned the boat under the lee of the breakwater, but I don't remember rowing that far. The trip back was a rollercoaster ride, the boat wanted to surf. She dug her forefoot in and skewed off to one side or the other. We were lucky and guessed the side right in order to compensate. When we got back to the schooner we left the boat astern for fear of tearing out another seat trying to get it on the davits. By evening the wind settled down some and we got the boat out of the water. Fixing the seat became part of a weekend job, and fixing the frames is part of an entire refit that my dad did for Bob almost twenty years later.

When we lost one of our life rings in Nantucket Sound, I was elected to man the port Whitehall boat to retrieve it. It was halfway through a week's cruise. It had been damp at the end of the previous week and through the weekend. The beginning of this week was a little too windy, so we never got to set the tops'ls to dry them out. We were on our way to Nantucket with a great southwest wind and maybe a two or three foot sea. Everything was going well with the schooner cranking under her four lowers. Being the boatswain at the

"A fall from the topmast -I'll never forget the look in his eyes, one of desperation and fear." (image by Dan Urish)

time, I was keeping an eye on the gear when I noticed the tops'l gaskets were fairly loose. I grabbed one of the crew and we went aloft to snug down the tops'l and t'gallant gaskets. It was a great day with a stiff breeze and from the tops'l yard looking down on the schooner it was magnificent. She ran along with a will and a bone in her teeth. The power underneath us was amazing, I felt like a cowboy riding his horse at a full gallop. We could see Nantucket, the Vineyard, and on the horizon the Cape far off. We stopped to take it all in. When we were done with the tops'l and t'gallant gaskets, we headed over to the main to take care of the gaff tops'l gasket. In those days it was common to get about the rig using parts of the rig. This day was no different and we crossed to the main via the spring stay.

In the beginning of the season it was my practice to check out the crew's abilities, so I knew who I could count on and for what. Unfortunately fate stepped in this day and threw us a curveball. I had gotten across to the main and up onto the weather shroud of the main topmast with my man right behind me. He did not choose to climb up to the shroud, but instead hung down at the crosstrees. He expected he could stand on the crosstrees, which he had done successfully at anchor when we were furling sail. This time, with the angle of the vessel's heel and the movement, he managed to stand on the crosstrees but did not manage to keep his balance. With a look in his eye of, "oh shit," and his hands stretched out for me or the shroud, I watched him in slow motion get further away from me. It did not matter how much I leaned towards him and stretched out, he was always just a quarter of an inch too far away but just right there. He went off of the mast towards the water on the port side.

I yelled out, "Man overboard!" Bob looked up from the wheel and then over to port and saw the splash. Bob tossed a life ring and I slid down the peak halyard to the deck as fast as I could. If I remember right, Joe was on as cook that year and he took his position in the weather main shroud as the spotter. In due time, we completed a Williamson turn and came upon our fallen shipmate. He had his wits about him and grabbed hold of a line we tossed him as the schooner came alongside him. We managed to get him on the boat, but he did not manage to hold onto the life ring, and so after another Williamson turn, *Shenandoah* was hove to and the port Whitehall boat, with me in it, set out.

The row to leeward was pretty easy—the sea wasn't so great that she surfed very much. I watched the schooner slowly sink away into the horizon until all I could see was the truck and occasionally the t'gallant yard. That life ring drifted pretty fast, and I was pretty far away from *Shenandoah* when I finally picked it up. Coming about and heading back was a comforting thought, but the pull was very hard and so very slow. I needed to stop rowing once or twice to bail the Whitehall out and I kept "catching a crab," which would jump the oar out of the oarlock. I thought of what I would do if I could not make the pull to windward. Up to this point everything had happened so quickly it was almost dreamlike.

In time, how much I have no idea, I made it back to the schooner. We got the Whitehall out of the water and cleared away for Nantucket. I have never spoken about this and have only written about it, other than in here, in my journal. I have read articles and seen this account mentioned but from a view less hands-on. I'll never forget the look in those eyes, one of desperation and fear. My own feelings of total inability to do something troubled me for a while and sometimes still do. I would never wish on anyone to have to look upon the eyes of a man in that spot, much less to actually fall from the crosstrees. We both went back to our work, although I went aloft alone to take care of the gaff tops'l gasket.

In all walks of life, there are risks in the professions we choose and we, each one of us, must choose whether we can live with the results of those risks should something go wrong. I believe there is no regulation that can be imposed that is better than one's own judgment. I fear there are too many doing what they have no aptitude for, but have passed some test or fit within some regulation, and so they're certified or qualified. This is a danger for many of us, passengers and crew.

Improvements and Innovation

IDEAS AND INNOVATIONS COME TO US ALL; to some faster than others. This is mostly because many of us are more creatures of habit than others. I am a creature of habit. I am reluctant to try new ideas or foods because, well, "it sounds complicated" or "it looks different." These are poor reasons, really, and the older I get, the more open-minded I have become. I do have a good friend that wants me to try lychee nuts, and I'm holding out. They look like eyeballs, man.

On *Shenandoah*, a vessel built on habit and tradition, innovation comes in odd places. Each year the crew, mostly new faces, brings to the schooner the latest and greatest of new ideas, but many don't apply or work out.

For a couple of seasons, young men with rock or mountain climbing experience have joined the crew. These fellows have done some really cool trips and I think it would be great fun to tag along with them. In working with these guys during fit out, the work goes easily. They have a great understanding of what it takes to deal with weight and conserving strength for the long haul while working aloft. They use webbing and clips instead of rope and knots. It is a little funny, because these mountaineers turned sailors have read about ropes and knots being the "old school" method. They want to learn it, and that is partly why they came to sign on the schooner.

For me, at this point ropes and knots have become something like my sheath knife: an old trusted friend, always ready and never

Evolution.

failing, though I have some friends that'll say, "Here—use mine, yours will barely cut butter." The webbing and clips are great, don't get me wrong, though when I first saw them I thought the webbing was thin for what they said it could do, and the clips looked flimsy compared with my bowline. But this innovation has gained a foothold, so that each year one of my ropes is replaced by a strap of webbing, and a clip replaces a knot. To a degree I must apologize here, for by letting this happen I have let the practices of seamanship slip.

At one point a simple idea changed how *Shenandoah* was handled on Sundays. After twenty-five or thirty years of going alongside the Coastwise Wharf every weekend to get power and water, someone came up with the idea of stringing garden hoses together and stretching them from the wharf out to the schooner. At about the same time the schooner was fitted with a generator and rheostat, which charged the batteries and provided the vessel with 110 volts of power while on her mooring or anchor. Whereas before this upgrade the genny could only change the schooner's batteries.

The Sunday docking routine was no good for anyone. Coming alongside the dock was stressful. More than once the starboard anchor got taken off the rail by being too close to the dock on the approach. The bo'sun was on duty all summer, because if it was his weekend off he had to stick around in case the schooner needed to be moved. Yeah, whoever came up with running the hoses out got my thanks.

I remember one time it had been windy for two Sundays in a row and we could not get to the dock. This was the third Sunday, and we were too low on water for the committed week's cruise. It was suggested to board the passengers and then head over to New Bedford to take on water there. That idea was nixed—why, I don't remember—but instead it was decided to get the schooner on the dock or close to it. So while it blew northeast, we let go of the mooring with the yawl boat under the stern and pushed towards the steamship dock. Once off the ferry dock, we let an anchor go just to the south of the dock. Then we paid out chain and let the schooner come stern-to, to the Coastwise Wharf. With the stern ten to fifteen feet off the dock the chain was held and two quarter lines were put out to the wharf. There is a great photo in the Black Dog Tavern of the schooner tied up in this way.

Over the years *Shenandoah* has gone through many changes, and it has been a lot of fun to witness and be a part of the change. *Shenandoah* was at one time, from what I've been told, a little more yacht-ish. Her booms and gaffs started out with painted white ends and varnish oil between. Then they got painted all white, but after a while they went back to how they started: without the varnish, just oil. The Whitehall boats had varnished sterns, rails, and interiors. The deck boxes were decorated with large diamond patterns in the tops. *Shenandoah's* color scheme has changed from white to black with shades of gray in between. I always thought she looked good with the gray, although I have seen her in all her colors and must admit she wore them all very well. While she was black she had individually painted gun ports, as well as an entirely white gun port strake. She's had a red stripe painted down the scupper strake, and she's been without any stripes at all. On her billet, originally, she carried an antique carved ornament for two years which now hangs in Bob's office. In the Black Dog Tavern, hanging over the entrance, is a billet that was carved by Carl Sprague and used on *Shenandoah* until 1976 when Travis Fulton carved the gilded eagle she carries as of this writing.

One of the biggest changes in *Shenandoah's* rig was the foremast head. It once was the same as the mainmast head, in that the trestle trees were the same length and it had two crosstrees. In an effort to brace the yards up sharper, the fore trestle trees were lengthened and a third crosstree added aft. The futtock shrouds and topmast shrouds were placed on the aft two crosstrees. This allowed the tops'l and course yard a better bracing angle.

In the early '90s the mast was altered again; a fourth crosstree was added forward of the topmast heel to rest the headstay on. This lifted the headstay off the lower yard and gave the headstay a sharper angle. Before this was done, the course yard would touch the headstay and twist the masthead when bracing up sharp.

After breaking one wooden dolphin striker which broke a jib boom, the striker was changed to the steel pipe it is now. Bob was upset over this change because the wooden dolphin striker was apparently a lovely turned spar. After a martingale let go and broke another jib boom, all the chain head gear was changed from

The Doublings.

1/2 inch to 5/8 inch. I think it was when I had the rig out the first time that a snout iron was added to the end of the jib boom. Bob was having trouble with the wooden shoulder being crushed on the end of the jib boom from all the tension of the head rig. I told him about a model of a Gloucester fishing schooner I was building and how the bowsprits or jib booms had this snout iron on them. I showed it to him in *American Fishing Schooners* by Howard Chapelle, and we got one made for *Shenandoah*. There's no longer a snout iron on the jib boom because the jib boom is now made of brownheart. It used to be Douglas fir, like all the other spars.

The chunky, square-cornered yokes for the topsail and topgallant were given more rounded-corner shapes. The original ones would tear the ratlines off the topmast shrouds when the yard was struck. In order to prevent this, the mate had to always remember to let slack the lee brace, but this didn't always happen. I remember as bo'sun re-seizing as many as eight ratlines on the topmast shrouds that had been torn off by the yoke on the tops'l yard.

The t'gallant leechl'ns, which now run through fairleads on the back side of the last crosstree, once led through the lubber holes. This was changed because the line would get pinched by the spreader at the most inconvenient times.

The gaff tops'l halyard was a single-part line when I started on *Shenandoah*, whereas now there is a whip on a whip system similar in the way a fish tackle is set up.

The doghouses were added to the schooner after Bob got married and had kids. He needed a place for the mate and babysitter. Before the kids, but after the missus, the mate was bunking in Cabin One. Before this change, he stayed in the aft cabin with Bob. The cook bunked in the fo'c's'le with the galley boy, crew, and bo'sun. In the fo'c's'le, the bo'sun had the top starboard bunk, with the cook in the port top and the galley boy in the bottom port bunk. The other three bunks were left for the crew. Yeah, that's right, only three crew in the day. Feel like a baby now, don't ya? Bob now, and for some time, has sailed with six crew in the fo'c's'le. The cook moved into the starboard doghouse when the sitter was no longer needed. In the day, the galley boy started on the Coastwise Wharf as a dock boy. If he showed interest in the schooner and sailing, he was given the galley boy job for the coming season. After a season in the galley, he could have a crew position. One hell of an initiation, I'd say.

One improvement, but maybe not for the long haul, is the reduction in the number of stanchions in the waist. It definitely cuts down on maintenance, but the longevity of the vessel is something I would consider. *Shenandoah* has once or twice been hit—and hard. With less timber in her waist, she may not be as resilient as she has been.

Altering the buntl'ns was something I always wanted to do on the tops'l. There have always been four separate lines, two to port and two to starboard, so that on deck you pull on two lines to bunt the sail up port and starboard. It was always necessary to "split your bunts" to get the slack out of the longer of the two. I proposed, as in *Young Sea Officer's Sheet Anchor* by Darcy Lever, Esq., buntl'n legs. This is a line that tied to the outer cringle on the foot of the sail and led up the sail and through the block on the mast. Make a bight of line here, and then lead down through the block and down the sail to the foot of the sail, and tie off the end. At the bight in the buntl'n, up at the block, there needs to be a thimble at least. I think a full-blown block would be too cumbersome. The thimble would have a line spliced on it that leads to the deck. This would make to port and starboard a single buntl'n on deck, so when pulled on, the buntl'ns leg in the sail would work as needed. The short buntl'n leg end would come up hard. The thimble would slide along this continuous buntl'n leg and the longer side would come up hard. The "splitting of the bunts" would happen by itself. A few small benefits to this renovation would be less line used, and less line to handle during fit-out or strip-down. Also, no need to "split the bunts" while striking the sail, which makes for less confusion and faster handling of the sail.

Other little details that I've been a part of consist of things like the foc'sle table and the storage bins under the doghouse bunks. The davit stays on the small boat davits were an idea I picked up out of some book. I seem to remember it was something about tying down a load on a truck. The old stays did not have the eyelet spliced into the standing part, so we would pull the end through the fairlead on the rail as tight as we could and tie a rolling hitch on the standing part. It would rain, and then everything would dry out, and those stupid stays were always loose. By putting the spliced eye in the standing part, you could lead the bitter end up through it and haul down on it, making for good tension.

The pudding booms used to be a constant bother, always sliding down the davit and being out of alignment. You could never get the lashings tight enough to withstand the stretch. So we made up grommets, and hung them from the cleats for the pudding booms to sit in. That ended the constant snugging and realignment of the pudding booms and lashings. This detail got worked into *Alabama's* gear.

We also had handles on all the hooks. The anchor burton, yawl boat falls, and Whitehall falls were all decorated with these elaborate or simple handles. Bob and I had noticed the detail on the *Lagoda* model in the New Bedford Whaling Museum. We were there one day shirking our duties, or was it doing research. Oh well, it was for a good reason I'm sure. After seeing them on the *Lagoda*, I took up Ashley's book to look for some ideas, and saw them in there as well. Bob asked if I could do it, and so we made some up for *Shenandoah*. On the anchor burton, it proved a most wonderful remedy to pinched fingers. Collaborating with Bob in some of these cases and initiating others all these years has really given me an opportunity to thoroughly refine my marlinespike seamanship as well as examine and work with the stresses and forces at work in a big sailing vessel.

Finishing touch.

Cook's Soup

WHEN YOU COME DOWN TO IT, no matter what it is you engage your time in, there is risk. We are forced to accept it if we wish to follow what we have engaged ourselves in. Risk is sometimes bantered away with boastful laughs, and many argue luck plays a major role, but some will say there is a higher power in control. Still others will argue that you are in total control of how things go and luck or a higher power have nothing to do with anything. Well, I am undecided on the matter. There are arguments for all three cases as I see it, but it is amazing that more people are not killed in, as Henry M. Plummer wrote in *The Boy, Me, and the Cat,* "Sport. The pursuit of pleasurable occupation which requires exposure to weather, judgment, skill of hand, foot and eye, never to be followed without a degree of personal risk. Under such classification I put Sailing of boats, Handling of horses, Hunting and canoeing, Mountain climbing. I know of no other purely sporting propositions."

Back in time.

In my time on *Shenandoah*, and the marine trade for that matter, I've seen things that would make the hardest skeptic believe in luck or a higher power. I think it is really delusional to argue that one cannot get into much trouble while playing with boats around the coast or inland waterways. So many things are out of your control and can go wrong, like a bad forecast or a brand new piece of gear breaking.

Having something dropped from aloft is one of the biggest mistakes anyone in the crew on *Shenandoah* can make. Gravity works on that object falling so well that I've seen a twelve-inch marlinspike hit the deck point first and drive in three inches. I have even seen a shackle pin land on its eye and stand in the deck. Sometimes what comes down from aloft is so surprising it's funny, not that we need to take up dropping things from aloft for laughs. But the grease pot that came from aloft and landed on the after house was, at the end of the day, quite humorous.

On *Shenandoah*, when we were becalmed for the day in Tarpaulin Cove, the mate or bos'n would issue projects to the crew. This one fellow was given a grease pot and sent up the main topmast to grease the spar, and the pot, about the size of a large coffee can, had gotten free. It landed on the after house right side up as if someone set it there, but the contents upon impact jumped out of the can. The grease covered a five-foot radius around the can, which included one or two passengers sunbathing. Whether the knot let go or the string broke, I do not remember, but it was a big mess.

Then there was the day a crescent wrench went through the galley skylight. Usually the first week of sailing is a hard one. The crew is new and there are many things to untangle in the rig. We were in the process of getting the mains'l set for our first sail of the season. All was going well until we peaked up. With all the noise on deck no one heard the wrench hit the glass. The cook came flying out of the galley yelling at the top of his lungs and waving

All home.

the wrench in his hand. Who was the ass who ruined his soup?! The whole thing is quite amazing, because all the skylights have gratings on them. When the wrench slid off the gaff jaws, it set itself up to go between the bars of the grating. It broke out a rectangular piece of glass the size of the wrench but not the whole glass pane. The wrench's flight ended in the soup simmering on the galley stove. It's a good thing the cook wasn't hovering over the pot testing or smelling his creation. From that point on I checked the gaff jaws twice, three times even, before I started to hoist for the first sail. The reason the wrench was there in the first place is that there are horseshoe-shaped irons that hold the throat of the sail to the gaff. These irons bolt in place on the gaff jaws and you need a wrench to handle the nuts. It had been forgotten by the crew member who had done the job. Yes, it could have been prevented, but to go through the grating like it did instead of being stopped by the skylight bars was beyond reason! If a higher power is in charge, he was proving that even the cook was not out of reach.

Yeah, I cannot say one way or other, but I'm open-minded. One incident I remember where the only one who was in danger of getting killed was the guy who made the mistake. I would also say luck did not have a part in this but for the fact that he was lucky I did not kill him. I had given a fellow the job of painting the fore boom and gaff tips white. This was during fit out so the boom and gaff were on their crutches. He was up on the spars painting the tips when he knocked the paint can off. It was like watching a movie in slow motion. The paint can spun in the air doing cartwheels, throwing paint as it spun. Its travel took it through an open saloon skylight and down onto the cabin table where it landed upside down. The paint ran off the table, dripped onto the benches and eventually the cabin sole. The paint was everywhere on deck, all over the walls of the saloon as well as three quarters of the cabin table. I needed to be restrained, for I was the reason his life was in danger. That mess took the rest of the day to clean up, and I needed the following day to cool off.

When playing with boats, big or small, there are so many things that are out of your control, it's not funny. You do everything in your power to make it safe and fun for passengers and crew. But if you really sat down and thought it through, you probably would not gamble against the risk without believing in a higher power or luck.

Great Wind Ships

S O MANY YARNS HAVE BEEN TOLD ABOUT WRECKS, gales, or hardship that when I was little, I could not understand why anyone would play with boats. I know now, from writing this book partly, it is just easier to write about the hard days. It takes less effort and imagination to write about hardship or something going wrong. Writing about a hard day is okay, and reading about them is exciting, but the good days on *Shenandoah* are equally etched in my mind. Some of them when I close my eyes I can see as if I was standing on the deck with the wind rushing by my cheek. Others are small fragments, bits and pieces, but a pleasant feeling in the heart and mind.

The day we made Mystic Seaport in five or six hours is one of those days where I can remember every detail. It was Monday with a howling four-lower northeast wind. The sea was running in Vineyard Haven Harbor high enough to put a damper on trips back and forth to the Coastwise Wharf. As is the custom for Monday, all morning we worked at getting the meats and vegetables on the schooner and stowed away. All the cardboard was crushed up, tied together, and shipped back ashore. Runs were made to Oak Bluffs for last-minute drink mixes for the passengers. We, the crew, were sitting around forward of the mast having lunch, talking among ourselves. We were taking bets on what would be the excuse for not getting underway on this incredible afternoon. The majority figured it would be too much wind, and one or two of us figured the Old Man would just be too late getting aboard. This banter was thrown around by carefree crew sitting forward of the mast with full bellies and delusions of understanding about things for which we had no idea. It is true, one or two "chances along," as the old coaster men would say, may have been missed for some reason or other but the reasons are only that of the skipper's concern. I was forward of the mast this trip, just a common seaman without any knowledge that in fifteen years I would be going with Bob again to Mystic, but in command of *Alabama*, Bob's other charter vessel, that had not yet been put together. I know now what it is to be criticized for what seems to be the unjust dictions by those who have no responsibility or understanding.

Before lunch was over Bob came aboard the schooner and summoned the mate. We in the crew were dying to know who the winner of the bet was. To our shock and amazement the mate ordered for the immediate stowing of lunch. He also wanted us to get the schooner "on the yellow line." This yellow line was a slip line we would put on the mooring ball in preparation for getting underway. It is a heavy piece of polypropylene that takes the place of the port anchor chain. We weren't quite finished with the yellow line when up alongside came Ralph Packer driving his tug *Corvus*. The deck man threw our mate a heaving line which a couple of us hauled in. On the other end was the towline that the mate made off to the bits. Soon *Corvus* took a strain on that towline and we slipped our mooring. The schooner started ahead and followed in tow down the middle of Vineyard Haven Harbor with a slight favor to the East Chop point.

"The grain ship" Kappel.

During the tow, orders were given to get the mains'l on and then the fores'l. We were just about in alignment with the West and East Chop lights when *Corvus* altered her course towards the west. Orders were given to get the outer jib and the stays'l on while the mate let go of the towline. The inner jib was set and sheeted in while *Corvus* was left in the spray, far astern as we rounded West Chop light. The schooner took the breeze over her starboard side and leaned into her task, building speed as she rolled along. It was a clear day with a crisp, strong wind, and we raced along with all the line and standing rig bar taut in this first leg, passing West Chop, bound for what appeared to be Tarpaulin Cove. The schooner would yield to the gusts and roll to leeward, where the sea would jump through the scuppers and flood the lee deck. The schooner pushed the sea before her so that the lee anchor was in foam. To weather, the bone in her teeth had consumed the hawsepipe.

Down around Tarps, the breeze came a little more on our aft quarter and the order to, "Lay aloft on your tops'l," was given. One of us in the crew jumped for the shrouds and ran aloft while the rest of us threw off the gear on deck. In time, "Ready on the tops'l," was heard from aloft with the quick and sharp reply, "Throw her off," given by the mate. The mate and bo'sun worked like dogs on the tops'l sheets till they heard from aloft,

45

"Starboard home," and "Port home." Almost instantly was heard, "Both home ready to hoist," and again sharp and quickly the mate yelled out, "Go ahead." Crew on the halyard leaned into the task of hauling on the halyard, when off in the distance from aft was heard, "Hold that." The skipper had spoken and from his place at the wheel had called the halyard. The mate then sang out without hesitation, "Hold that," "Make that," and "Coil down."

The added sail drove the schooner like she was trying to outrun the wind. Her master slacked sheets and worked his vessel to give him all she could. She leaned into her task and made the quarter wake grab the keel and rudder of the yawl boat hanging high on her davits. Forward the lee anchor was no longer in foam but now green water. The scuppers were playing with the sea, throwing water at the passengers trying to sit in the center of the schooner over the saloon skylights. In one or two of the gusts the schooner would yield and the port Whitehall boat would float in its grips and form a rooster tail coming off its keel.

We cleared Cuttyhunk and were bound for the west. We the crew speculated again, will it be Block Island or Newport, or even Mystic? Bets were made in ignorance of the immense amount of strain the schooner was under while she crashed along trying to please her skipper. Bob and *Shenandoah* were racing or working to beat someone or something, maybe time itself. For the skipper and his schooner were pushing as if for a loved one's life. The old banks fishermen would never have stood a chance beating Bob and *Shenandoah* to market with the way they were charging along.

Buzzards Bay Tower, Sakonnet Light, and the Newport Bridge all went by to windward as *Shenandoah* ran on, out of control but yet not. With Watch Hill gone by we were now in Fishers Island Sound. The breeze slowly lightened up, but the skipper's will was for speed. The t'gallant and the gaff tops'l had been set under the lee of Watch Hill. In Fishers Island Sound with no sea, *Shenandoah* slid along as if she were greased. We

The schooner Shenandoah heads home after a good day's sail – "She slid along as if she were greased." (image by Dan Urish)

approached Mystic and the wind let up as we turned into the Mystic River. The wind slowly died away, so the yawl boat was dropped and the canvas was taken in as we pushed up the river. The bridges were met and opened as if it was planned, which it was, and to the minute.

Once at the top of the river, we were given a space against the dock next to the schooner *Brilliant*. It was after hours and the seaport museum was empty. It was like a ghost town but not in the Old West. Instead, it could have been "Boston, New York, or Buffalo" to quote an old chantey. The cook was in the process of getting dinner out on to the cabin table as we came alongside the dock. After dinner many of the passengers and all of the crew went for a walk around the seaport. The last of the setting sun was starting to fade as we walked along the seaport docks. The twilight was coming to an end and engulfing the masts and spars of all those great wind ships in darkness.

What Would the Old-timers Say?

THE LOWER YARD ON *SHENANDOAH* IS 11 INCHES in diameter at the truss iron and 53 feet long—solid Douglas fir. We all speculate on how heavy it is when it's dressed and ready to go aloft. There's the truss iron and bands at the ends of the yard that are all made up out of 3/4 inch thick flat stock, 3 inches wide. There's 4 feet of 1-1/4 inch chain that takes the weight of the yard when up in place as the sling. Then there's the jackstay made out of 5/8-inch rod, which runs the entire length of the yard, along with numerous eyebolts 18 inches apart that fasten it to the yard. Wire gear, braces, lifts and footropes, which are all ½-inch plow steel wire. The anchor burton chain is always on the yard when it goes aloft. The burton itself, unless it has already gone up to be used for some task around the deck, I usually send up with the lower yard. Otherwise, it takes two men an entire morning to get it in place. Actually, I can't say that I really want to know how heavy that damn thing is. It's good enough to say it's heavy. My biggest concern has always been getting it up in place or back on the deck without breaking something or killing someone; "The skipper takes a dim view of either one." (Johnson)

When I started on *Shenandoah*, it was the practice with the yards to take the lowest one down first in the fall; consequently, the highest one went up first in the spring. I can remember leaving the schooner at the end of a work day with the t'gallant and tops'l yards in place but the lower yard not yet up. To myself, I thought how the old-timers must be rolling over in their graves. I also remember once the lower and tops'l yards were off and the t'gallant was still up. Not only were the old-timers rolling over in their graves, but they were crying their eyes out that year. When the task became my responsibility to house or set the yards, I changed this method and put them up or took them in in their setting or striking order. My reasoning for this was that the yard underneath you gives you a staging to handle the gear of the yard over you–not to say anything of the aesthetics of it from the beach. Now I have admitted many times that there are dozens of ways to skin a cat and everyone has his own little way of doing it. So I can't judge, and neither should anyone else what is the right way or wrong way to skin cats or rig up 108-foot tops'l schooners, or any other vessel for that matter. All I ask is that you recognize that this is my take on it and, yes, it involves a lot of not reinventing the wheel.

In preparation for hoisting the lower yard, the yard itself can be dressed with its footropes, tops'l sheet pendants, and anchor burton. The lower braces need to be sent aloft and shackled in the main shrouds, with the braces fleeted out to the base of the fore shrouds. The lower lifts need to be taken to the foremast cap iron and

Pass it forward, son.

lengths of line bent onto their bitter ends so that the wire pendants can be brought to the deck. This means that the lifts are fleeted out also. An outhaul needs to be rigged to the end of the jib boom to prevent the yard from riding the face of the foremast. I have always used the outer jib halyard for this. Short lines need to be secured to the waist, then sent around the yard and back to the waist so that when the yard is lifted it does not swing to the center of the schooner and sweep the deck clean of its skylights. A halyard needs to be rigged to hoist the yard up into position. All these things go on basically at the same time, but with all this preparation done, the yard can be hoisted aloft and bolted in place fairly quickly.

If we start with the lower yard on the deck to port, this means the tops'l and t'gallant are laying on the deck to starboard. We put the yards on deck like this so the schooner is in trim for the winter. We rig the halyard so that the hauling end comes down to the starboard side of the schooner. Otherwise, the hauling end will be in the way of getting the yard off the deck. The halyard to raise the lower yard consists of the 1 1/2" three-strand nylon line, which is also used as the heel rope when setting or housing a topmast. There are three snatch blocks employed: one on the lower yard, one in the center tied in place with a 1¼ inch braid strop (that used to have a thimble seized in the center of it), one in the forward end of the starboard trestletrees on the foremast. The bitter end of the nylon line is tied into the port trestletree eyebolt. This knot should be something small and strain-resistant. A bowline is good but can be too long; I have always used a buntline hitch for this job. The length of this knot is important because when the yard is up getting bolted to the futtock band, if the knot is too long and there is stretch in the strop holding the snatch block to the yard, the halyard will two-block and you will not get the height needed to hook up the truss iron or the chain sling. The third snatch block is placed in the waist of the schooner. This placement has been in different places over the years, but for all the work I've done I have placed it in the gun port, just aft of the foremast shrouds.

Rigging this block in place is easy. The fender board is hung overboard so it lies across the gun port. It can be tied to the last deadeye and through the hole for the forward Whitehall davit in the rail. Then, with a strop around the fender board and through the gun port, you can attach the snatch block.

Put your backs to it!

To recap, the halyard is running from the capstan to a snatch block in the gun port on the starboard side just aft of the fore topmast backstay, up to the starboard foremast trestletree where there is a snatch block on the eyebolt, down to a snatch block on the yard and then back up to the port trestletree eyebolt, to be made off.

With the halyard rove we can now concentrate on the rest of the gear needed to keep the yard under control. Because *Shenandoah* has a good bit of rake in her spars, it is necessary to keep the yards forward of the mast.

I've always done this using the outer and inner jib halyards. The outer jib halyard is rigged on the end of the jib boom so that the hauling block is attached to the lower yard at the pick point in the center of the yard and the working block is shackled to the base of the outer jib stay or strapped around the jib boom end. This places the hauling end of the outer jib halyard coming off the yard, so a snatch block on the end of the bowsprit is needed to redirect the hauling end of the halyard back to the deck. Once the lower yard is up off the deck, this halyard can pull the yard forward of the vertical pick point and forward of the face of the foremast. The inner or outer jib halyards are more than adequate on their own to keep the yards off the mast while they are being hoisted. For the most part, the man tending this line is slacking out and keeps the yard about 6 inches to a foot off the mast. If we were striking the yards it is necessary to put the two halyards on top of each other for the power. The rake in *Shenandoah's* masts is so much that if you were to just lower the yard it would end up fifteen feet aft of the foremast once it got to the deck, not to mention the tangled mess it would make on the way down. So the job on the way down becomes one of pulling the yard forward of the mast.

For the initial lift of the lower yard you must have at least two lines, one at each end of the yard tying it to the waist of the schooner, because the yard dressed in all its gear is too heavy for the crew to keep from swinging to the centerline of the vessel. I have always taken these two lines and dead-ended them on the rail, say, at the base of a deadeye lanyard, then gone around the yard and back around the deadeye lanyard so that

Go ahead on your halyard.

the yard can be slid through the loop made. If necessary, you can slack this line to move the yard toward the centerline of the schooner. Once the yard is moved so that the truss iron is just forward of the mast, these lines used to hold it off the skylights are not needed any longer.

With the lower yard still on the deck but with the truss iron alongside the mast, I usually attach the starboard lower lift to the iron at the base of the yardarm. That means that the lifts for the lower yard are up in place and shackled to the foremast cap iron. They are fleeted out so that the wire pendants are on the deck. In order to fleet these lifts to the deck, lines need to be bent on to the bitter ends of these lifts; they're not long enough on their own. The starboard lower brace is also rigged and fleeted out to the foremast shrouds. The yard is 5 to 6 feet off the deck at this point, and the outer jib halyard is holding the yard forward. The starboard brace is shackled onto the yard and the port yardarm is being manhandled on the deck back by the saloon skylight. With the starboard lift and brace on the yard, hoisting is resumed and the yard is sent aloft, starboard yardarm first, until the truss iron is about halfway up the foremast.

Throughout the hoisting, the starboard lift is taken up. This maneuvers the yard to stand on its end, under complete control. Once the yard is almost vertical, the port yardarm should clear the rail cap and swing forward of the base of the port foremast shrouds. It is now time to attach the port lift and the port brace to their respective iron at the base of the yardarm. With this done, the yard can be squared, so the starboard lift is slacked off and the port lift is taken up. Also, the braces are manned so that the yard is controlled and not allowed to swing freely. From here to the futtock band, the halyard is hoisted, the outhaul is slacked out, and the lifts are taken up; also the braces are manned. Once the yard has made it to the futtock band, there can be a little jiggling involved to get the truss iron and futtock band hooked up. This depends on many variables, such as: yard too close, too far away, yard rolled in lifting strop, etc. To try to describe it all here would take another book. Besides, I need to leave something for the next guy to figure out. We will say that this is a perfect job and the futtock band and truss iron are joined. This means the outhaul is "all off" and more strain is put on the halyard so the chain sling for the lower yard can be shackled to its iron, spanning the trestletrees on the forward side of the fore topmast heel.

With the lower yard in place, the lifts can be adjusted so the yard is square to the mast. The braces can be taken up to make the yard square to the centerline of the vessel. The outhaul can be sent down to the deck, and the halyard that hoisted the yard can be broken down and rove to hoist the tops'l yard.

"Yard Home"

WITH THE LOWER YARD UP AND IN PLACE, it's now time to hang the tops'l yard. In the early days I sent the tops'l and t'gallant yards up with only their foot ropes and Flemish horses, but these days they go aloft with everything from sail to leechl'ns and gaskets. While the lower yard's halyard is being rove for the tops'l, there can be some crew putting the tops'l together on deck. If you move the yard up against the skylight coamings it will give you the room on deck to bend the sail to the jackstay. It's necessary to move the t'gallant either aft or to the other side of the vessel to make the most room for the sail on the side deck. By bending sail on deck, you save half a day in work and get a nice tight head rope with a well- centered sail. There is some risk and challenge in getting the yard up without ripping or snagging the sail, but it's no more or less than sending the sail up by itself. If you have ever bent a square sail on a yard while aloft, even on a calm day, you know what it takes. With two fellows bending the sail on the yard, someone can be dealing with the foot ropes and Flemish horses. Someone else can reeve the bunt-lines and leech-lines through the sail and fairleads on the yard. T'gallant sheets and tops'l clewl'ns can also be rove by another member of the crew. All this is happening on deck, while aloft, someone is re-leading the halyard to hoist the yard.

Sometimes when one does something for a very long time they become good or accomplished at it, working all the details down to a well-choreographed dance. This is nothing more than making every trip ashore or out to the vessel, aloft, or to the deck productive. There is a great deal of forethought needed to achieve this successful dance. I have gotten a reputation for being proficient and have managed to put all three yards up in one day, fully rigged with sails. The crew is hustling. My crew has always been willing to give me everything they have. If it weren't for their hard work and dedication, it would not be possible to get so much done in one day. So, truth be known, all these years my crew really have rigged *Shenandoah* in the record time of two days and deserve the respect; I have only directed the traffic.

The fellow aloft reeving the lower yard halyard for the tops'l needs to bring the halyard from the forward side, at the eyebolt in the trestletree, down and under the shrouds of the mast, then back up the aft side of the mast. It then needs to be led to the port side of the spring stay and to the bee-hole in the topmast. The bee-hole I use is the one just under the mast band at the top of the topmast shrouds.

When hoisting the tops'l yard, one looks for the halyard going from the deck aft of everything straight to the bee-hole in the topmast for the tops'l halyard; from there, forward of everything and down to the deck on the side where the tops'l yard rests. With the bitter end now on deck, I tie it to a shackle on the center band of the yard. The outer jib halyard, which was used as the outhaul for the lower yard, is taken and used again as the outhaul for the tops'l. The two lines that held the lower yard to the rail and prevented it from crashing into the skylight coaming are also used on the tops'l yard for the initial lifting. These were the two lines that were just sent around the yard so the yard can be slid through the loops. As with the lower yard, they're no longer needed once the yard is forward of the mast and ready to be stood on end. As with the lower yard, the tops'l yard is picked up off its blocking on deck and slowly moved forward of the base of the mast. Unlike the lower yard there are no braces or lifts to attach at this point, so the yard is just stood on its end and sent aloft.

Day's end.

I said there are no lifts or braces to shackle at deck, but there are aloft. The tops'l braces are sent aloft to the mainmast cap iron and fleeted out so they can be sent across to the foremast doublings. This can be done with a heaving line between the two masts, or two men and a line between them as they go up the shrouds. One guy can even do the whole job by fixing the brace on the main, then overhauling the brace and taking the brace pennant up the fore shroud. No matter how, the braces need to be ready at the foremast to receive the yard.

The lifts are on the yard in a special way. They are both shackled to their ends on the yard, but the end of the yard that is going aloft first must have its lift's loose end tied to the iron on the end of the yard. The other end of the yard needs its lift's loose end tied to the center of the yard.

So let's say that the yard has been hoisted and is standing on its end with the port yardarm at about the inner jib stay. The yoke is at about the crosstrees and the starboard yardarm is down by the upper end of the lower shrouds. Okay, the yard should be stopped so the two crew aloft can shackle up the port brace and the port lift. You may have forgotten, but I started this story with the lower yard to port, which means the tops'l was on the deck to starboard. This means the port end of the tops'l goes aloft first. Now, with the yard's end at the top of the topmast shrouds, you have in front of you the port lift because its loose end is to be tied to the iron. Whoever goes up the topmast shroud takes the brace pennant with him and shackles it on as well. The yard can now be hoisted some more, as well as let to go square. She will not just fall square, because the coils of ropes made from the tops'l gear get off center, putting the yard out of balance. This is a help because you want a controlled squaring, not a hard, crashing one. With the yard hoisted so the yoke is above the topmast cap iron, you can stop the halyard. The crew aloft can take the starboard brace and shackle it to its place on the yard, and the lift, at the center of the yard, can be carried up the shrouds to where it shackles on the top of the topmast shrouds. This will square the yard, so the outhaul can be slacked and the yoke will rest against the topmast. The parrel beads can be hooked up and the halyard slacked so the weight of the yard rests in the lifts. From aloft, you'll hear the boys sing out, "Yard home," at which point everyone starts on the t'gallant.

The t'gallant is not much different than the tops'l or the course yard in how it's set up and sent aloft. *Shenandoah*, unlike so many of the other tops'l schooners around now, has a "standing t'gallant yard," meaning the yard is up on the mast and worked in place. *Pride of Baltimore II, Amistad*, and many others have an "on the fly" t'gallant, meaning that it is set from the deck when they need the extra sail. This is not the only difference that sets *Shenandoah* apart, and I mention it only because so many aspects of the ships are similar. What I'm writing here could be used as a guide on many other vessels.

With the t'gallant, one of the biggest differences is getting to the fore topmast head and the spider band. In the old days, or at the start of my career on *Shenandoah*, someone in the crew would climb the backstay from the top of the topmast shrouds, to the masthead. This fellow would have a line with him long enough to at least reach the top of the topmast shrouds where another crew member would have gear to tie to it. The crewman at the masthead would hoist the gear up and shackle it into place. This would include the halyard to hoist the t'gallant yard. After being the guy who climbed the backstay and sat on the top band for one too many times, I got sick of the job; no one else would do it. "It's too high," "It's too heavy," "I'm scared of heights," and, "I can't do that," is all I heard. Sometimes I was not interested in trying to explain what needed to be done, so I would do it myself because it was faster.

Well, it is true that necessity is the mother of invention. What I learned to do is leave a line in the bee-hole of the t'gallant halyard and ride the yard. The line was synthetic, and long enough to make it from the middle band on the topmast up and through the bee-hole at the masthead, then back down to the middle band, where it was made off. This line is set up when the yard is sent to the deck in the fall. Before the chain pendant of the t'gallant halyard was removed, I would marry a piece of 1/2-inch nylon three-strand to the end of it. This did two things: it made it easy to lower the chain pendant to a man in the shrouds, and to reeve a line up through the halyard bee-hole at the masthead. With this line up in place, you could marry the inch-and-a- half hoisting halyard and reeve it through the sheave on the masthead without needing to go aloft. Once you are done putting the t'gallant on deck, but before you remove the hoisting halyard from the topmast masthead, you marry the 1/2-inch line to its end which, once again, allows you to lower the hoisting halyard and reeve the 1/2-inch synthetic for the coming season. I always used to wrap the two ends around the topmast backstay and then tie the ends in the topmast shrouds. This prevented the line from slapping the mast and chafing itself during the course of the winter.

The t'gallant is not as rigging friendly as the tops'l because there are no shrouds with ratlines to work from. This becomes a problem when getting the lifts and buntl'ns shackled in place. The t'gallant is set up on deck the same way as the tops'l is with its sail, clewl'ns, and leechl'ns. The braces are also set up the same way as the tops'l, but both lifts have their loose ends tied in the center of the yard. The outer jib is still used as the outhaul, but remember to put the hauling block on the yard, not the jib head block.

So, we're going to say that the t'gallant is hanging on its halyard with the port yardarm just above the inner jib stay. At this point, the port t'gallant brace is shackled in place. This done, the halyard is allowed to hoist so that the yoke is about 6 inches above the inner jib stay or mast band. The halyard is stopped again and the starboard t'gallant brace is shackled on from out on the tops'l yard. The t'gallant can now go square and be slacked against the mast to have the parrel beads hooked up. At this point, the outhaul has been slacked off, the braces are being manned, and one of the two crew members aloft climbs up onto the yard. The yard is then hoisted to the masthead, where the man riding the yard shackles the lifts, buntl'ns, and outer jib halyard onto the mast band at the top of the topmast. With all these things shackled in place, the yard can be lowered into its lifts, at which point, someone aloft will yell, "Yard home!" That, of course, brings the end of a long, hard day on *Shenandoah*.

Now of course there is still a lot of work that needs to be done. The hoisting halyard needs to be dropped to the deck, all of the tops'l and t'gallant gear needs to be dropped to the deck and rove through their fairleads. Some of this can be done at the end of the day depending on how much time is left. But I'm going to touch on one or two things that make life a little easier, or at least I thought it did.

One of those things is the hoisting halyard and using the 1/2-inch nylon line on it to lower it to the man in the shrouds. This also will reeve the 1/2-inch line, and give you something to reeve the chain pendant for the t'gallant halyard. But remember, we put the outer jib halyard at the masthead. The bitter end has to be overhauled from the forward side of the yard and sent down the aft side as well as aft of the crosstrees to the last pin on the port foremast pin rail. If you tie the bitter end of the outer jib halyard to the 1 1/2 inch nylon hoisting halyard, one is slacked down to the deck while the other is being rove to the deck, and it can be done by crew on deck. This is also true for the fall when you're taking the schooner apart. Everything is done in reverse. You would hoist the hoisting halyard aloft using the bitter end of the outer jib halyard, and so on.

The last thing I will touch upon is the dropping of the gear. A lot of crew over the years have gotten confused with how things are rove from the yards to the deck. Actually nothing is really rove through anything except the batten in the lower shrouds. All the gear for the tops'l goes from the blocks outside of the topmast shrouds right to the fairlead batten in the lower fore shrouds. The t'gallant clewl'ns do the same thing. The leechl'ns, however, go from the blocks down and through two fairleads on the aftmost crosstrees of the foremast doublings, then to the batten in the fore lower shrouds. I always dropped the gear with the yards square because you can see the straight leads. The tops'l and t'gallant halyards are the only things to be rove through the lubber holes. Well no, the fore peak halyard does too, but nothing else.

Reefed Topsail

YOU KNOW THOSE TIMES IN LIFE where a very notable thing happened? You can remember all the details of the day; what you were doing, where you were and who you were with. For many of us September 11, 2001, is one of those days. We all knew someone directly or indirectly involved with that infamous day. The entire New England region became a family. A mass of people, perfect strangers, instantly bonded together.

As you may have guessed, I was on *Shenandoah*. We were anchored in Padanaram outside the breakwater. It was a rough, windy day, and we needed to move the schooner because the forecast was for southeast overnight, and Padanaram is an open harbor to the southeast. It was Tuesday. Bob did not want to go back into Holmes Hole. Ducking into New Bedford was not an option, either. Because of the forecast, he had decided upon Marion. For a good part of the summer we, the crew, had been ribbing the Old Man about reef points in the tops'l without lines. "Why have the sailmaker put them in if you're never going to use them?" We had also been on him about not reefing down.

Well, on September 11, *Shenandoah* went for a sail in Buzzards Bay with a reefed tops'l. After one or two hitches up the bay setting the outer jib and striking it in order to get the schooner to come about, we suggested trying the reefed tops'l for fun. There was a good bit of resistance from Bob before we got it set. "It's too far aft to make much of a difference." "It's really too windy for sail that high." "It's too much trouble." But he finally consented and let us play with the sail.

Goose wing.

We the crew, had already made up reef lines for the sail and had put them in. We had planned on setting the sail one day with the reef in. We had figured, of course, it would have been mutinous, but tying a reef in and setting it on him with some excuse was worth the trouble it may have caused. That day was a gift. Setting that sail reefed turned out to be a really good sail choice for *Shenandoah*. She no longer needed the outer jib or the tacking tackle to make her come about, even with the sea running as big as it was. *Shenandoah* had the power to cut down the sea that before would bring her to a stop and make her miss stays. She also did not have any extra heel with the sail so high off the water. The tops'l is built so that when the reef is tied in and the sail is set, there is no need to hoist the tops'l yard; it sets nicely the way it is.

It's not possible.

As we played on the deck of our time capsule, the outside world was raging war on itself. The cook was the messenger for all of us on *Shenandoah*. He emerged from the galley where he was working on lunch with the news that a plane had just been reported crashing into one of the twin tower buildings. We were dumbfounded. "It's not possible!"

Puff pulled the radio he was listening to out of the galley and set it on the cabin house back by Bob at the wheel. We listened to the newsman giving a blow-by-blow account. I now know how all those people who tuned in the radio so many years ago to listen to a newsman telling about aliens taking over the world must have felt. Of course that was *War of the Worlds,* a radio theater show, but this was real. Passengers on the schooner started getting calls from loved ones, "such-and-such may have been on that plane." "How is this possible?" I heard someone say.

Our glorious morning of play in a time so distant from reality had been made into a dream and memory. The entire rest of the day, week, month, fall, and year were engulfed in terrorism talk and fear. We never had another opportunity to play with the reefed tops'l. It is just a memory now, for me one with so many unanswered questions.

That day taught me that the little moments in time where we can block out reality and live in a moment of our own dreams or desires are to be cherished, because you never know who or what may rob us of the moment. That sail is such a distant memory now. It's like a ship engulfed in one of those smoky sou'wester fogs far off on the horizon.

Kindred Spirit

IN THE SUMMER OF '92, WE PARTICIPATED in Tall Ship Boston. The big rendezvous are great fun, and it's really wonderful to see the mass of vessels all congregated in one spot. It can easily lull a hopeless romantic mariner into dreams of yesteryear. That particular year, there were vessels of all sizes and types floating around the New England coast. We went through more gunpowder that summer than we had since I

Boys and their toys.. (from the author's collection)

came on board the schooner. I think we even replaced the flag halyards twice because of the frequent saluting to vessels we spoke around the Vineyard and Buzzards Bay. Jamie and Brooke, two of Bob's sons, spent a good bit of time on the boat in the early nineties. One of these seasons was the summer of the model boats. It was a good stretch of time with a lot of things going on and the three of us, or at least I, had a lot of fun.

The summer of the model boats was an attempt to get the crew to work together and be engaged in their surroundings. I decided we would all build model boats as a crew project. I put a maximum length on the hulls of about twenty-four inches and a week's time on the construction. The models were going to be simple, and at the end of the week I had planned a race. We would fine-tune them during the second week. At the end of that first week we had a great model race in Tarpaulin Cove. At the end of the second week, we had a better race in Kettle Cove. A couple of the guys in the crew really excelled and had a lot of fun with the little boat models all summer long. It taught everybody design, sailing dynamics, engineering, and a little artistic winging it. All in all, it was a success.

Jamie was one of the guys that took it up and ran with it so strongly he got his older brother Robbie interested. They later won the model boat race in Menemsha many years in a row with model boats they built. Once or twice they would ask for my opinion or help, but they really didn't need it. They were doing pretty well on their own. Jamie and I raced our model boats all summer, fine-tuning them here and there depending on wind and sea conditions. He had me hands down. I, like the English, had trouble diverting from traditional ideas, where Jamie did not. Enough said—we know where modern design has taken us.

Now I'm really not one for picking one guy out of a crowd. I've worked with a lot of boys and girls over the years on the schooner and many talented people, men and women, in the marine industry. But working with Jamie on the schooner that summer was fun. He had such a happy-go-lucky attitude, and what a PR man! One of the fun, stupid things we did the summer of Tall Ship Boston was to truck the mast for the length of the Cape Cod Canal as the schooner was towed through to Boston for the rendezvous.

Trucking is to sit upon the topmost point of a mast. Many vessels have a disk fitted to the top of the topmost mast. It protects the end grain and houses the flag halyard sheaves. On *Shenandoah,* this truck is about

12 inches in diameter and 2 to 2 ½ inches thick. *Shenandoah's* main topmast truck is littered with the initials of many of the mates that have served her. Anyway, as you sit atop the mast you wrap your legs around the mast. It can be an insecure feeling, but it's also a rush. While sitting there we waved to everyone on the shore as we were towed along through the canal. My butt was some sore by the time I got down, but the cheers, whistles, and applause were all well worth it.

During one of the week cruises that summer in Buzzards Bay, we heard out of the blue what sounded like a cannon going off, and then shouts from forward. We were going along nicely on a starboard tack with the tops'ls on. Bob, Jamie, and I

For posterity.

59

were aft by the wheel enjoying the sail and making small talk, when one of the fore topmast backstays parted. Bob wanted to get the t'gallant off fast. Jamie, with a look in his eye, turned to Bob and me and said, "Lay aloft my heroes bold," (Nelson Burns, "The Yankee Man-O-War"), then turned and ran down the deck as fast as he could. I, with a bit of shock and a laugh from Jamie's statement, took off after him. He took to the shrouds like a cat after a mouse and I went for the t'gallant halyard. With the halyard let go and the yard in its lifts, I took to the shrouds and met up with Jamie on the yard. Jamie, upon my arrival, was out on the windward side doing what he could to muzzle the sail from flogging. I jumped to leeward and took up the fight there. At one point Jamie yells over, "Put your backs into it, lads." There were, of course, just the two of us on the yard, but we were fighting a squares'l on a wind ship with broken gear and well, you know, it was the moment; it had his imagination.

Bob always likes to say about someone who was of a kindred spirit that, "He was on the same wavelength." I'd agree. Jamie has the spirit in him, and that spirit comes from the top on *Shenandoah*. Bob made us feel like we were a part of his family or company. He drove home that we had a vested interest in *Shenandoah* and her wellbeing, or at least that was my experience. Bob is not a micromanager; he took me for my word and let me prove to him and myself my abilities or inabilities. He's a fair judge of character; hell, he let me sail with him all these years. Though we (he and I) have clashed once or twice on the choice of a new crewman, it's as has been for as long as men have sailed. The mate and skipper each know better, and this is even more true once they start to act like an old married couple. This reminds me of an old story about Zeb Tilton and Charlie Sayle on the old *Alice S. Wentworth*.

They were going along down Vineyard Sound, and Zeb was upset with Charlie and his poor headsail trimming. Charlie was yelling back at Zeb about falling off and not pinching the old *Wentworth* as much. This barrage of insults passed back and forth between the two men for a while. Zeb would yell at Charlie to mind his own business and take care of his end of the vessel, and to leave him (Zeb) to his end. Charlie would go off on a rant saying Zeb didn't know what he was doing or how to sail. At some point there came from forward a crash and a clatter that made Zeb jump with fear and shock, yelling at Charlie, "What in the hell was that!" Charlie replied that he had anchored his end of the vessel, and that Zeb could do whatever the hell he wanted with his end.

With Bob and I, we never came to that. He can be tough, but I think it comes from his passion for the history of the sea and his love of his baby, *Shenandoah*. Bob is a very passionate fellow with regards to *Shenandoah* and the traditions surrounding her. I would almost say he sees himself as a watchdog, protecting the history and traditions of it all. He can be very hard and opinionated about things, but there is a passion behind it that most don't see unless they know him. I've known Bob since I was very young, so I've known him as a family friend before I knew him as an employer. Same with his boys; they have always been extended family, not such-and-such's kids. I realize this by itself has provided me with a much different experience on *Shenandoah* than many others have had over the years. Aside from this, *Shenandoah* has been very dear to me because she is like that first love. She is that woman that gave me the chance to prove I was more than a boy.

Shenandoah is Bob's creation, his vision and a dream come true. Bob is *Shenandoah's* protector, custodian, and person. This last one is the most important, in my opinion. To have a person makes all the difference with everything from houses to animals to even people. We have all seen the effect of "having a person." It's a patina, the glow of use and care. It's that house where the kitchen table is not as swept clean as if it was a showpiece in a store, but not as piled on as if it's a dumpsite. Or a boat that is not polished enough for a boat show in Newport, Rhode Island, but nothing is so bad you would be scared to sail her. Or a dog that's gray and slow but has a look in her eye of a puppy.

I think Old Lodge Skins was right or had a point when he said, "The soul of the thing comes to life with the touch of this type of person. All things have life and the human being sees it. There's an endless supply of white men, but there has always been a limited number of human beings." (The movie *Little Big Man*)

"Still No Bob!"

FOR ALL THE TIMES I HAVE DEALT WITH THE TOPMASTS on *Shenandoah* or any other vessel, I have always rigged the heel rope in the typical way. This means the heel rope dead ends on the masthead cap iron and reeves through the bee-hole in the butt of the topmast. Then it goes back up to a block on the cap iron, and from there to the deck. At the deck, many things have been done on *Shenandoah*, from utilizing the eyebolts in the deck for the peak and throat halyard fairleads, to using the top of the chain plates and even the gun ports. I never liked the eyebolts or top of the chain plates because the direction of load the heel rope makes puts the wrong angle of pull on these points. Remember, a fairlead bisects the angle of the line you're re-leading. It's important to keep in mind the load angle at a fairlead point. Both the eyebolt and chain plate are strong but they are both designed for an in-line strain. Using them as fairlead points compromises their strength and may deform them. For the heel rope on the main topmast I've used the gun ports just forward of the main shrouds, and for the fore, just aft of the fore shrouds. This gives me a nice fairlead that I can then take forward to another fairlead tied in the gun port just opposite the capstan for the main, but with the fore I go directly to the capstan. With the heel rope rove in this way, the lead from the gun port to the capstan is not too high off the deck, so the crew can step over it while working the capstan. More importantly, it's strong.

Before a strain can be taken on the heel rope, the topmast shrouds and backstays must be slackened. By only loosening the shrouds, you still support the mast while aloft. It used to be that the shrouds did not need to be slackened because the fid was a two-inch-diameter steel rod that sat on the trestletrees, and if you took a strain on the heel rope, you would move the mast enough to slide the fid out. Now, the fid is a large wooden block that is made to rest on the trestletrees, but part of it sits between the trestletrees. The main topmast must be lifted an inch or more to clear that section of fid between the trestletrees, and the fore must go up 6 inches to clear the headstay. This also means with the fore top mast, the outer jib stay must be removed or left off, depending on whether the spar is being hoisted or lowered. The outer jib stay is a fixed length without "bending room" in the jib boom to get the height necessary for the fid. With the fid out, the mast can be lowered to the first iron, where there are some choices to make.

The two middle irons on *Shenandoah's* topmasts are split so that they can be taken off without being slid off the top end of the spar. The top ones are solid and need to be slipped off from the top of the mast. This middle iron does not need to be removed from the mast but can be left there, and the mast will slide through it once the bolts are loosened. This "leaving the middle band in place" has the advantage of also leaving the topmast shrouds, which allows you the luxury of having an easy means to ascend the masthead where one usually sits to house the topmast and feed the gear by the doublings. On the mainmast this is more important than the foremast because the main trestletrees are shorter fore and aft than the fore and don't have as much room for standing while handling the gear.

That was never as obvious as it was in '89, when we took the main topmast down. Geoff was the mate. Apparently, he and Bob had noticed during the summer the old mast would take a bend to leeward whenever the gaff tops'l was set with a good wind in it. In the vicinity of the middle band, the stick had gotten soft, so Bob had decided to take it down and replace it at the end of the season.

The top of the topmast snaps off, sweeps down and ends up dangling precariously over the main deck! (image by Dan Urish)

Geoff was on the lower masthead and I was on the crosstrees clearing the gear from snags. Doug was slacking the heel rope at the capstan. We had just gotten the spar down to the first band when Geoff sang out, "Shit! Look out!" Before I noticed what he was talking about, a very dark, grease-covered hunk of wood went by me barely twelve inches away, followed by a tangle of wire. The top of the topmast, some twenty feet of solid Douglas fir, twelve inches in diameter, had gotten free of its counterpart, the lower end. It took up on its headstay, dangling between the fore and mainmast, hovering over the middle of the deck where Doug was tailing the heel rope on the capstan. This is why there is a kink in the wire of the main topmast headstay.

We all had our different experiences: Geoff being crushed by the spar as it rolled over his back, me being nearly knocked off the masthead as the wire I was holding went slack, and Doug at the capstan with half a mast hanging over his head and the other half resting in his hands on the tail end of the heel rope. All of us were too scared to let go of what we were holding onto, but we knew we had bigger problems to deal with. Doug was the first one to make a move and got the heel rope tied off quickly so he could get out from underneath that stick hanging over his head. When I realized I wasn't harmed in any way, I spoke to Geoff to make sure he hadn't been crushed to death by the mast.

The mast had gone off to port and took up on its headstay, then rolled over Geoff's shoulder and down the starboard side by me. Once we had managed to get ourselves back together, we worked on getting the top half of the spar down to the deck. We left the butt end lowered where it was and concentrated on the top end, figuring that at any moment it would slip out of its iron and hit the deck.

What we ended up doing was one hell of a hair-raising project. I got the short straw, in that I had to go out on the spring stay and down the topmast headstay to the mast and get lines on the mast. We then took to the main and foremast heads, and with them we took a strain. Once the load of the mast was off the headstay, we disconnected the headstay from the foremast cap iron. Then we slacked away on these two lines, and slowly lowered the topmast down to the deck.

Geoff got a lot of mileage out of that story. Well, we all did, really. For a long time the lower end of the busted stick was on the dock out in front of the Black Dog as a kind of bench. As amazing as it may seem, no one saw what happened with that mast falling down. We must've spent the entire day dealing with it, and how it was that nobody ever saw what we were doing, I just don't know. Maybe they just didn't know what they were looking at. Geoff and Bob were quite pleased with themselves, apparently. They had figured out on paper the top half of the topmast would clear the deck, and so it did.

This all happened with only three of us on the boat: Geoff, the mate; Doug, I believe was his name, the bo'sun; and myself, the boy. All the rest of the crew had gone home or back to college. We three down-rigged the schooner that year, taking all the running rigging down and the sails off. That year we did not get out for a sail drying day either, so we had to hoist the sails on the mooring to dry them. The mains'l and fores'l were a job to get up. The three of us went back and forth between the peak and throat halyards. As the sail was lifted the weight became greater and greater, so in the end, I was sent up the shrouds and I hung off the halyard while Geoff and Doug pulled. The most important thing I learned that season was that despite the size and weight of everything, if you had a good grasp of blocks, tackle, and leverage, you could get any job done with only a few hands.

So back to housing the topmast. At this point, it is a good idea to get a line on the butt end of the topmast to keep it off the lower mast. *Shenandoah* has a lot of rake in her masts and the topmasts want to slide against the faces of the lower masts or slide off the sides. With this line attached to the butt end you can control the lower end of the topmast. With this guideline in place, you can continue to lower the mast to the second band or top band, whichever you want to call it. The top band and truck can be removed and the mast can be lowered to the deck.

Once free of the trestletrees, lowering the topmast to the deck can be done in many different ways, from a line to the trestletrees, to lines and men in the shrouds. More recently I have used two shackles, but in the past I have always used a line around the heel rope tied to the topmast head. This line is really quite simple and handy. The shackles are more handy and simpler, but the line is basically tied to the mast and looped around the heel rope where it passes by the mast on port and starboard. The line is loose around the heel rope so that the heel rope slides through the loops. When the masthead clears the trestle trees, this line is basically holding the head of the mast to the heel rope so the top of the mast can't tip over. With the head of the topmast tied up this way, you can put the mast on the deck without needing a man aloft. Once the butt end is on deck and tied down, you continue to slack out on the heel rope. This allows the head of the mast to be lowered to the deck without any extra line.

Yankee ingenuity.

You could work the butt end of the mast forward along the deck and let the masthead come to rest at the base of the lower mast. This is what I've done with the fore topmast because otherwise the heel rope will put up too much of a fight. If you let the heel rope lower the head of the fore topmast, then it will make too much friction in the trestletrees as the head goes aft. But if you work the heel aft along the deck and let the masthead come straight down the foremast, it makes a fairlead for the heel rope between the trestletrees. No matter how you move the masts around on deck, the point is that if you tie the heel rope at about the masthead band, it makes it much easier to handle the topmast going up or down. These days I no longer use a loop of line but seize two shackles, one per side, to the topmast. The two shackles are better points for the least amount of friction than the bare rope. You must remember to seize them with the pins against the mast; otherwise the heel rope will work on the pins and unscrew them. This would be bad.

I remember when I first did this on *Shenandoah* years ago. We were in New Bedford to take the lowers out for repairs and maintenance. The schooner and I spent the winter tied up just inside Old Wharf at Kelly's. Bob and I had been working on getting the schooner de-rigged. We had gotten the heel rope rigged the day before in preparation to drop the topmast this day and Bob was going to bring help when he came in the morning. He was staying at Captain Elton Hall's house, an old friend of his, and now mine. I was staying on the boat at Kelly's. Well, I had gotten up early and was going over everything to make sure all was well and ready. I busied myself with picking up and coiling lines while waiting for Bob.

Now at ten in the morning, he was late and I got it in my head that gravity does most of the work. Also, as long as the mast is in the cap iron and between the trestletrees it cannot fall. So I started, lifted the topmast and got the fid out. Not too bad, still no Bob, then I slacked the heel rope to the first band. Not too bad, still no Bob, and again slacked the heel rope to the second band. Still not too bad and still no Bob. At this point, I had it in my head that with the head of the topmast between the trestletrees it could still not get out of control. So I lowered the mast.

Now by this point I recognized that if the head of the mast was tied to the heel rope, then I could get the butt end on deck. With the butt of the topmast on deck, I could get a gantline on the head of the topmast and lower the head. So, still no Bob, I tied the masthead to the heel rope and lowered the butt end on deck and tied that four ways. Still no Bob! I was standing back looking over what I had done when it came to me that if I slacked the heel rope a little more, the head would lower—no gantline required. So I tried it, and it worked, though I had a lot of friction, which was probably for the better, because it kept it all moving slowly.

Well, now I had the topmast at about a forty-five degree angle when Bob showed up with Robby, Jamie, and Chip. That put an end to my job. Bob was shocked and amazed. I said, "It was no big deal." which has gotten me in more trouble over the years than I care to think of. I have a friend that has shortened "no big deal" to "nobd." I showed Bob how I got the idea: Darcy Lever's book *Sheet Anchor,* where there is a similar approach which I used as a basis for what I did. Well, after all the explaining and pats on the head we all finished the job and laid the mast on deck, then broke for lunch.

After that day, many things changed for me and in my surroundings. I became far more confident in what I was doing, but it was what happened around me that was what I really was proud of. From that day 'til today, the fishermen and yard hands no longer just passed me by. Instead they would nod or wave, even say hello. There were men who even went so far as to make it a point to stop by once a day or so and ask how I was getting along. In a shipyard like Kelly's that caters to workboats and mega yachts, an old wooden sailing vessel is just in the way.

About a week after the topmast job, I was out on the end of the bowsprit dealing with the sheaves in the cap iron for the inner jib stay. I was having a hell of a time with them and they just would not budge. Being out on the end of the bowsprit did not help. I had just about given up when two yard guys came up to the dock where the bowsprit was overhanging and set up scaffolding under me. Then a guy from one of the fish boats came with a cutting torch. Someone else showed up with big wrenches and the whole job was made so simple. The bolts came out with the sheaves and everyone and everything went back from whence it came. It's how the whole winter went, and to a degree, my life, little things here and there. I tried to return the help where I could, but it never seemed to be necessary. I had earned my salt that winter in many regards.

A Pain in the ...

FOR SUCH A LITTLE STICK, THE JIB BOOM IS A PAIN to deal with. It is all dead weight with nothing over it or under it to get help from unless you hire a crane. When I had to deal with housing it there wasn't a bee-hole in the butt end, as there is now. We used to use a strop around the butt end cinched up underneath the cleats for our heel rope block. The spar is longer outboard of the bowsprit cap iron than inboard, making it bind in the cap iron.

A pain in the...

The only thing I've found that works half-way decently is putting the outer jib halyard on the outboard end of the spar. When housing this is very helpful, because it lifts the weight of the spar and draws the spar into the deck. When setting the spar, this makes the heel rope and halyard work against each other, making the job even more difficult than it already is. Unfortunately, there is no other way to support the weight.

I've only taken the jib boom in with the fore topmast up. The angle from the foremast head out to the end of the jib boom is too great to efficiently support the weight while trying to house or set the jib boom. I'm sure it could still be done, but I just don't want the job.

In dealing with the jib boom, I have always removed the shrouds and bobstay. Well, let me clarify this by saying I remove the shrouds and Martingale backstays from the catheads. This removes a lot of back pressure on the heel rope, especially for the first bit of the housing job, when the spar must be sent out to clear the heel chock before the jib boom can come in. There is barely enough slack in the shrouds with the bottle screws all backed off to get this done. I have never taken the shrouds off the end of the jib boom first. There is too much weight in the chain shrouds to deal with on the end of the jib boom, with nowhere to stand or sit or hang.

Once the spar is housed so its tip is to the cap iron on the bowsprit, I remove the bobstay and shrouds. The bowsprit is a good working platform to deal with the weight of the chain. The iron band comes off at this point also, but the snout iron will pass through the cap iron. At some point before now, I have put the outer halyard on the balance point and moved the heel rope block to the same place. The jib boom is much easier to handle this way. The spar can now be brought in to the deck and the job is done.

The bowsprit has only been removed twice in the vessel's time. The spar is solid fir, 24 feet long and 18 inches square at the knight heads. It is one of two such spars that were cut from a timber at the Pigeon Hollow Spar Co. yard. *Mary Day* was given the other bowsprit. Pigeon made all the spares for *Shenandoah* and Bob has told me about the Old Man's office and yard. "He sat in front of an old roll top desk and over the desk

Part of something bigger.

on the wall was a framed line drawing of *Mayflower*. He was one of the consortium members and he built the spars for her." Sometimes the line of history is just too cool for words. I'm going to throw in another little detail here, even though it does not fit. It's just too cool to leave out, but while Bob was doing the alterations to the *Joe Lanes* lines, he was consulting with Walter McGinnis, who worked for Thomas McManus, who worked for Dennison J. Lawlor.

The first time the bowsprit was out of *Shenandoah*, Bob used his work boat *White Foot*. She had a derrick on her stern to do salvage work with, and Bob used her to move *Shenandoah's* spars on and off the vessel. Bob sold *White Foot* in 1986, so the bowsprit has not been out for thirty years.

Before removing the bowsprit, remember there is a bronze pin in the butt end that goes through the bits. This holds the heel down to apply pressure on the bobstays. If you strop the bowsprit around at the heel chock for the jib boom, then you will be a little to one side of the balance point; it would be good to move the strop to a point 3 inches aft of the jib boom heel chock where it would become balanced. Really, there is not much to removing this spar. It's very straightforward.

Masting & Rigging

AS WITH ALL THINGS, WHEN SOMETHING IS NEW, one has a tendency to spend more energy trying to keep things nice. *Shenandoah* was once no exception. In the early days, Bob would take everything off the schooner; the small boats, the varnish, deck boxes, sails, galley pots and pans, and the bedding. Even the booms, gaffs, and yards went in his concrete garage ashore. This was done with one of Bob's work boats, *White Foot*. Now I realize this little bit of history may not be important, but it was a detail that helped me realize the answer to a problem. It's also been the ace up my sleeve to win numerous bets.

The first time I helped Bob get the lower masts out of *Shenandoah*, I needed to get the booms and gaffs off their saddles and down on deck. It took some guesswork for me to find the balance point of these spars to handle them easily. I had heard Bob tell stories of his picking the sticks up with *White Foot's* derrick and taking them ashore season after season. He knew the balance point on every one of these spars and eventually I found it too, without any measuring or relying on memory because… they're marked. All you need do is run your hand along the top of the spars and you'll find a screw head.

Unfortunately, the fore boom is no longer marked because it's a new spar and the screw was not put in. I never got a chance to mark it. The main boom is no longer marked on the top, but now on the bottom. That's because years ago, the boom was rolled over because the tongue had been put on upside down when the new jaws were put on. The spar, after so many years of hanging there, had taken a pretty good swayback in it also. By rolling it over, it fixed both problems; in a season or two, the spar became straight again. So, this is why you need to run your hand along its underside to find the balance point. I've always been amazed at where the balance point is, for it's never where you think it would be.

The jib boom was never marked and I don't remember where I used to pick it up, but something's gotta be left for the next generation to figure out. It's a little thing; we used to put it on our shoulders. With the bowsprit, its balance point is 3 inches aft of the heel chock for the jib boom. If you pick it up at the heel chock so the strap is just around the beginning of the chamfer on the edge of the bowsprit, the inboard end will be a little heavy, but nothing one man can't handle.

With balance points being the topic, let me tell you about the lower masts. These two spars are solid Douglas fir, about 70 feet in length. They measure 20 inches at the mast partners (the deck) and 16 inches at the trestletrees. There are four shrouds made of ¾-inch galvanized wire per side. The spring stay and headstay are also 7/8-inch wire, with the headstay doubled. In taking the lower masts out of *Shenandoah*, I would like to relay some helpful hints that I have learned through the four times I have dealt with removing and stepping these spars. The prime pick point for these masts is a point down from the futtock band equal to the length of the masthead, cap iron to futtock band. You'll find this spot is perfect because it leaves the spar in the same attitude (i.e. the same angle of rake) that it is in when the spar is in the vessel. The mast is very butt heavy and cannot be handled on the ground. In order to lay the spar down or pick it up from the ground, you need a sheet

of plywood under the butt end to rest the tenon on. Because *Shenandoah's* masts are so raked, it's more important to pick the spars out or set them on this angle. Otherwise, the masts will jam in the partners because the mast steps are so far forward of the partners. Now, this aforementioned pick point is only good with the spars dressed and topmasts off. If you don't remove the topmasts, then you need a damn big crane to take the weight. I would not do the job without removing the topmast because the masthead is not meant

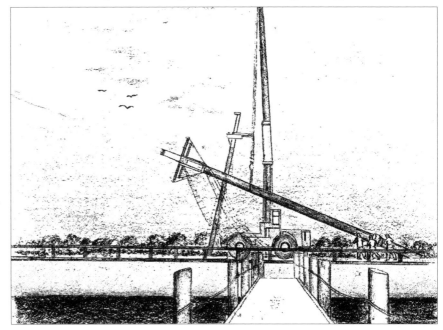

Taking off the butt heavy mast dockside, a matter of delicate balance.
(image by Dan Urish)

to support the weight in a horizontal attitude, to say nothing of trying to separate the topmast and lower mast once on the ground. Why anyone would pull the spars with the topmast in place is beyond me. It would make the job much more difficult, though I will say I have seen crazier things done. The rake in *Shenandoah's* masts and the pick point I have suggested makes for a little more work for the crane operator, but I have yet to run across an operator who has scratched any varnish.

When I was doing this work, all the gear on *Shenandoah* was in good standing. The mainmast, once the spring stay had been let go, did not need a temporary headstay. It would stand until the shrouds were let go and the mast could be lifted out by the crane. If those involved would be more comfortable, they could use a dock line, as I did the first time I had to deal with this job. Unfortunately, the dock line had too much stretch in it to pull the masthead forward, making insufficient slack to get the pin out of the spring stay. Also, with the spring stay being horizontal, there is too much weight.

What did work well, and what I've used over and over again, is a ¾-inch line tied onto the spring stay's thimble. It needs to be long enough to make it down to the deck while being rove through the spring stay bail on the foremast head. It's a waste of time to lead this line through a snatch block tied around the masthead. The direction of the pull ends up too much on an angle instead of directly in line with the spring stay. By going over the bail and straight to the deck, the pull is directly in line with the spring stay. There is some friction, but not enough that the crew can't overpower it with the tackle on deck. On deck, a four-part tackle is tied to the end and anchored to the base of the chain plates just under a deadeye. With the crew hauling on this tackle, the main masthead is pulled forward through the spring stay, relieving the pressure on the spring stay shackle so it can be undone. With the shackle undone, the pressure can be let off and the four-part tackle disassembled.

Then I, at the masthead, would slack the spring stay against the mainmast using this line. The line is let fall to the deck and someone else can tie it up at the base of the mast so the spring stay doesn't flop around in midair. This method could be used in hooking up the spring stay as well, just done in reverse.

Now mind you, this job is being done on the fore masthead, not the main masthead. We are in the process of taking out the mainmast, but the job of disconnecting the stay is being done on a mast still stayed off. This is wisdom learned from a colleague's misfortune. A good friend of my father's lost his life while trying to unhook a spring stay on a big vessel up in Maine many years ago. I have worked with some who will argue while having the crane attached to the mast the spar can't fall over. This is actually not true. I have handled poor spars that have been standing for a very long time, only to find they collapse under their own weight once horizontal. I even had a mast that looked like it was going to pull apart at the mast partners. The tenon was stuck in the mast step and the mast wedges we could have scooped out with a spoon, they were so rotten.

When I pick up a mast I try to pick it up just above its balance point so that handling it on the ground is easier. It is possible to pick a mast up by its top or close to it, but in many cases that means having to go to the masthead to hook up the crane because spreaders or shrouds are in the way when slipping an eye or loop up that far on a mast. If you are trying to pick masts up so they are butt heavy, then you have figured the bury of the mast into the equation of balance. If the bury breaks off at the deck where many old masts are bad, then the mast will be top-heavy and, despite the crane, will fall over. In *Shenandoah's* case, there is too much rake to pick the mast up by its head. The mast would jam up in the partners because the mast step is so far forward of the partners. Just more work and inconvenience. In the case of the mast coming apart at the partners, I luckily had the forethought to tie the base of the mast four ways. I got lucky and it stayed together, but at the deck that mast was rotten three-quarters of the way through.

I've had some tell me that setting up the extra gear to uncouple a spring stay or headstay is a waste of time because all you need to do is have the crane operator pull the mast forward. This doesn't work in many cases. The boat is in the water and you just drag the boat forward. Dock lines stretch and you're now putting unknown pressure on dozens of different things. It may be a small bit of extra work but it's worked for me and I have got a pretty good track record.

Thanks to many people, like my parents, Bob Douglas, the folks at Gannon and Benjamin, Beetle Co., and the Coast Guard just to name a few, I have been able to practice and keep alive what Henry Bhondell once took for granted. Henry was a fourth generation rigger who put the rig in *Shenandoah* for Bob the first time. Bob has told me about the man, rigging twenty four-masted coasting schooners in his lifetime. Bob would say, "He could put a splice in one-inch wire as fast as I could tie my shoes." The t'gallant halyard block on the end of the chain was given to Bob by Henry. It is said that the block was a jib sheet block on a big coaster.

I have looked at *Shenandoah* and her rig as a direct connection to a living textbook. I have studied what Henry did over and over. For example: there are no bottle screws (turnbuckles) in *Shenandoah's* headstays. Henry could make a piece of wire the length he wanted it. He also knew sailors would be out on the bow sprit and jib boom handling sail. By not having a bottle screw on the stay, the jib can be stowed very close to the bowsprit or jib boom. This may not seem important, but when things go wrong and you are out there dealing with a sail flogging in a hard wind, having a sail you can get on is better than one over your head.

In dealing with vessels that have more than one mast, I have always worked aft to forward or forward to aft, depending on whether the spars were coming out or going in. In most vessels that have more than one mast, rigs are designed so that support for the aft mast comes from the forward mast. *Shenandoah's* mainmast, for example, is entirely supported by the foremast through the spring stay. If you were to take the foremast out of her but leave the mainmast, it would be important to rig up a temporary headstay to support the mainmast. This also would be true if you were to take the jib boom and bowsprit out of her and left the fore topmast up; the fore topmast relies heavily on the jib boom and bowsprit to support it. There is an order of things concerning the masting and sparring of vessels.

The foremast in *Shenandoah* is handled in the same way the mainmast was. I have always used a similar tackle setup to haul the headstay and relieve tension on the headstay shackles on the gammon iron. With the spring stay, I go directly to the stay with the hauling line. With the headstay, I hang a gun tackle on the stay with the hauling block on the gammon iron. On the hauling end of the gun tackle I add a four-part tackle like on the spring stay job. With this setup, you can create the power to pull the mast ahead and get the shackles apart.

Loyalty and Duty

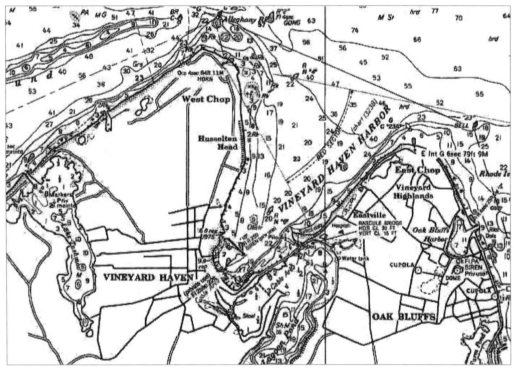

BEING AT THE MERCY OF THE ELEMENTS—wind, tide, visibility, and sea—can put a damper on where, when, and how long a day sail or a week trip can be in the charter business. I have been on trips when we have sailed great distances, and others where we never left the harbor. For example, during one weeklong cruise, we stayed one night on the mooring, the next night in Husselton Head, then moved over to Eastville. After that night we went to Holmes Hole, and then back to our mooring in Vineyard Haven.

Holme's hole.

As a mariner, to be able to read the signs and signals of the weather is a valuable art. A sailor who cannot read these signs may come to grief someday. In this day and age of sophisticated equipment, I feel we rely on gadgets a little too much, and not enough on gut or our ability to handle the gear or read the signs of nature. Computers or devices are only as good as what humans program into them. Also, life at sea is harsh on electronics, and corrosion is an ever constant and insidious aggressor that can strike at the most inopportune time. Yes, computers are getting better, and someday we will no longer need to think for ourselves. As skippers, it is our job to use all the information and tools at our disposal to make the best decisions. I believe we still need to rely on our gut and to be educated in the signs and ways of the old coaster men.

On *Shenandoah*, with the threat of a hurricane in the forecast, we would shackle up to the ball in Vineyard Haven as soon as the hurricane was reported to have passed the Outer Banks. My parents would have the carpenter shop cleared out and have planned out where their cutter *Ampelisca* would go to ride out the blow. These two men (Bob and George) have been criticized for "jumping the gun" or being overly cautious. But they have both encountered forecasts gone horribly wrong. One or two of those forecasts I can vouch for and so have learned to be as cautious.

I remember one time on *Ampelisca* when we were cruising in the fall. We had put into Cuttyhunk's outer harbor with a forecast that said southeast wind and rain for overnight into the next day. It never went southeast but was flat calm 'til about 2:00 a.m. when it came up northeast with a driving rain. To say it was rough was an understatement. By morning we had 250 feet of chain out on one anchor and 150 on a second. The sea rolled over *Ampelisca* like she was a half tide rock, but I'll leave the rest of that story for another day, or maybe another book.

I have ridden out a number of hurricanes on *Shenandoah*, though I never liked it because my loyalty was with *Ampelisca* and her skipper, but I fulfilled my duty on *Shenandoah*. In Vineyard Haven, *Shenandoah's* mooring is quite large. The anchor is a 5-ton army mushroom, with one shot (90 feet) of 2-inch stud link chain on that. This leads to 40 feet of inch-and-a-half stud link chain to a mooring ball 2 feet in diameter where we shackle in with the port anchor chain, which is ¾-inch stud link.

We would add stops and lashings to all the sails, stops on the halyards like jib and peak, so the wind could not grab the line and pulled the stows apart. We would put wedges in the jaws of the gaffs to make them tight on the mast, as well as tie the throat halyards off the mast to stop them from beating the spar.

The yards were never taken down on *Shenandoah* nor the sails taken in. I remember one blow, I think Hurricane Bob in August '92, where the black skiff, which my dad and I built in 1982, had nowhere to go that was safe to keep the boat. Bob would spread the small boats around the harbor to have means for getting to the various vessels of the fleet. Anyway, the black skiff had nowhere to go, so we put it on the rail of the schooner. We had to put the starboard Whitehall on deck and took the davits out of the rail so as to have room. We used the main and fore throat halyards to lift the skiff and worked the boat up the side of the schooner.

Most of the storms were not much because of the direction they took: along the coast. The island made a good lee. I remember being full of fire for one hurricane. I had this idea to see if what Irving Johnson said in his movie *Around Cape Horn* had any truth to it. Not to say I did not believe him, but I never let the truth impede on a good story, so why should anyone else? Well, I "hung down" off the fore topmast shrouds and yes, the wind was strong enough to hold me out but I did NOT "flap like a flag." I was not the only nut. The cook was with me; we were both hanging there. The wind in that storm of Johnson's must've been one incredible blow and yes, "leech sliding" is possible, also.

Bob has tossed around the idea of going into New Bedford when a hurricane is forecasted or if we can't make it back to the mooring in Vineyard Haven. That would be a safe place to hole up for a hurricane but we have yet to do it. Why, I'm not sure. It may be his gut telling him it's not necessary.

Sailing Qualities

A S TIME WENT ON, I GOT MORE COMFORTABLE with Bob and his vessel. I started to look at the whole thing in a more analytical way, watching the boat and skipper working together, which is very much like watching a dance. Sometimes Bob leads, and sometimes *Shenandoah* takes the lead.

She is not, as I call it, a buoy boat, which is to say fast or tight in stays. *Shenandoah* takes about four of her boat lengths to come about. *Alabama*, Bob's second schooner, and one I have commanded for Bob, is night-and-day different from *Shenandoah*. The large tacking radius and slowness in stays of *Shenandoah* can be

Old and the new.

troublesome. In a big sea she can fail to come about because too much momentum is lost with the sea pounding on her flare. Many harbors are off-limits to her because of the lack of maneuvering room. *Alabama*, on the other hand, can tack inside *Shenandoah's* tack and sail on or off her mooring in Vineyard Haven Harbor, whatever the wind direction. She is handy enough to sail off the Coastwise Wharf as well as up to Bannister's Wharf in Newport, Rhode Island, both things I have done with the boat. She is really no different to handle than any other large common yacht.

On the other hand, *Shenandoah* can do things that *Alabama* cannot. The schooner is a great wind vane. She sails on her mooring or anchor so slightly you can barely see it. Being such a weathervane she will drag back in a straight line, sail on or off. Many boats I've sailed fishtail as they go astern. They will get off on a tack as they go astern and will drag the anchor with them instead of going straight back. In order to stop the fishtail you must let out chain, get the vessel to calm down, and then start over. With *Shenandoah* you can just drag back till you are where you want to be. If sail is on, she can be steered to go in a direction while dragging back by tying the main boom to one side or the other.

Shenandoah will turn on her heel as if she had a spud at her stern post. If you leave the mains'l off and set the fores'l only, then set the stays'l at "short stay" and on the break set the outer jib to the opposite side you want to turn to, she will fall off and spin on her stern post. She will be three quarters of the way off the wind before she starts to make headway, and with the wheel hard down. She will continue falling off till she is dead downwind. In this last quarter of the turn, she will only make half a boat length of headway from her original position. Of course you need the room required for her radius to fall off in this manner, but that's true of any vessel. She will do this without the foresail on and only the stays'l, but not as quickly; also, she will do this with the main on, but again, not as well.

After watching and being a part of this maneuver, I once asked Bob why he does not sail off his mooring in Holmes Hole (Vineyard Haven) when the wind is from the southeast, south, or southwest. He stated that there is not enough room and she makes too much sternway. After talking with him, it came to light that he has always thought along the lines of a "standard takeoff." In Edgartown, a "standard takeoff" was never used, with the southwest wind and lack of room. After a good part of a summer's talk and planning, Bob consented to try sailing off the mooring in Vineyard Haven. The first time, there was barely enough wind to keep the booms out, and we had to have a line from the aft quarter to the mooring ball so she would not go astern. This is a consideration to keep in mind if there is not enough wind to blow her bow off and start momentum during the maneuver. All she will do is drift once she's broken loose from the bottom. My friend now brags about sailing off the mooring unless it's northeast or there is no wind at all, and sometimes adds, "It's all Dom's fault."

Another nice feature of *Shenandoah* is her airbrakes. Yes, I said airbrakes, but not like on a semi-truck. I know this is hard to believe but is very true. All topsail schooners have them. For that matter all vessels with squares'ls have airbrakes.

I have been aboard the schooner when Bob asked for the tops'l to be set while rounding to an anchor in Nantucket Harbor. I have also heard many stories of sailing into Nantucket with the squares but no headsails, round-to and backing the squares, then letting go the anchor and taking in the squares, all in one fast but graceful motion.

We used to sail up the channel with all sail set to get in fast and be out of the way of the ferries. The schooner was always moving fast and as we rounded Brant Point Light, we would strike the heads'ls and tops'ls in that order. Sometimes the schooner would be moving too fast and would want to range ahead beyond where we normally anchor. If *Shenandoah* was full of power and looking like she was going to overrun Bob's mark, he would call for the yards to be squared. One of us in the crew would run aloft to prevent the sail from being snagged or ripped when the mate and bo'sun hauled on the sheets. The sail was never hoisted, only sheeted and usually clewed back up as fast as gotten out. The effect was instantaneous, but there was always a fear of something snagging which would have thrown the schooner into a tailspin.

Talking about sailing up channels reminds me of the day Bob shot the mooring. It was a day sail with adults on board. Why he chose to, to this day I'm not sure, but Charlene Douglas and Harold Summers were on—I remember that. Bob was all keyed up as we made the approach from the outer harbor. We were on our way in and setting up to anchor by the nun "6"N. As we rounded up, he changed

Smokey s'west.

his mind and tacked, putting us on a heading for the fishing pier at the north end of Packer's. We ran in with five lowers and no squares. Headsails were taken in on the approach. It was quite the maneuver, sailing *Shenandoah* up into the head of Vineyard Haven, a very confined place for a big vessel without internal power. I found out after or later that day that it was only the third time Bob had done this.

One other wonderful thing about *Shenandoah* is her gentle jibe. This jibe is so controlled that one man can handle the mainsheet no matter the wind. This is due to the great amount of rake in *Shenandoah's* masts. The booms swing in a pendulum form created by the diagonal from throat to clew. This swing has a great sweep to it, making the booms travel from port to starboard in a fair sized arc, unlike a vessel with plumb masts where the boom travels in a perfectly flat plane from port to starboard.

Another benefit of this rake is *Shenandoah's* headstays are very tight and without much sag when the headsails are set. If you look at her from athwartships, you will see the shrouds are pulling on the masts in an aft direction, forcing the mast to bend back and load the headstay. The headstay starts out fairly loaded just because of the rake. *Alabama's* shrouds lead straight down, requiring her to have running backstays to give her headstay tension. This added rigidity in the rig of *Shenandoah* makes her able to withstand shock like in a jibe.

Shenandoah's ability to do tricks is not nonexistent. Over the years I've heard some incredible stories like Bob going in to Vineyard Haven with bare poles and clubhauling to pick up his mooring during a northeaster, but I'm going to leave them to folklore. I can say I've been aboard when Bob sailed up to his mooring in Vineyard Haven. I've been told it has happened only three times in all the years Bob and *Shenandoah* have been together. Unlike coming in to an anchor, the mooring is an exact spot you need to hit. To judge where a 170 ton vessel is going to come to rest and make the spot of a steel mooring ball is good, to say the least.

Well, during the summer of '06 I had gone out to help with *Shenandoah's* fit out and also fit out a 35-foot Alden cutter by the name of *Atea*. It turned out I was to sail *Alabama* and see firsthand how different she is. Through friends, I had acquired *Atea* from Sven Goff's estate. Sven was an acquaintance of mine on the Vineyard. I had been introduced to him when I first started on *Shenandoah*. He and I would talk about boats and boat models and sail the models on the waterfront. He was an incredible sailor that I wish I could have had more time with. His reputation with the ocean racers *Ondine* is legendary.

Once *Atea* was in the water and *Shenandoah* was sailing, I made ready to head home with *Atea* and my Seabird yawl. While making ready for the trip home with one of the two boats, Bob asked me if I could skipper *Alabama* for him. He had just relieved the skipper he had hired and told me it would be temporary. He was in the process of looking for a man to do the whole season.

Well, this did not sit well with me for I had only been on *Alabama* for one day sail and knew nothing about her. I told Bob my concerns, but he just patted me on the back and said, "It's easy. She has training wheels," meaning two big 671 diesels under the deck. This did not comfort me and I did not tell Bob that I don't really know how to use engines. I know this may be hard to understand, but using engines is a totally different mentality. For my whole life engines have been troublesome. My own boat, *Sea Y'awl*, had no engine; my parent's boat, *Ampelisca*, had an engine that was too small to be of any use other than for docking maneuvers without any wind. My parents' first boat, *Nostalgia*, had an engine that ran only when it wanted to, and *Atea's* engine was seized up from sitting unused.

Then, of course, was all that experience while working on *Shenandoah*. I truly believe an auxiliary sailor does not think about or handle his vessel the same way a non-auxiliary sailor does. Anyway, with my friend Bob, I've always had a hard time saying no and so I agreed, telling him, "I'll do what I can."

After making arrangements for *Atea* and *Sea Y'awl* to be kept on moorings in Vineyard Haven Harbor, I turned my attention to learning how to sail *Alabama*. Another statement that may be hard to grasp but I believe vessels and boats have personalities that need to be learned. Thankfully, *Alabama* came with a very capable crew. If it weren't for them, I would have never looked as capable a captain. They truly were the brains behind the operation, and dare I say they were really in charge. I've been so lucky to have such competent friends and colleagues to work with and know over the years.

Hanging with a friend.

I ended up sailing her for the whole summer and I never filled the fuel tanks once. I don't know whether Bob could not find a man or was happy with his choice in me, but I'm glad I got the opportunity to work with the boat and her crew.

Ever since the *Alabama* was commissioned, the various skippers Bob had hired took her great distances. Naturally, with two large engines your field of operation is much greater in a week than if you had no engines.

Bob complained about this often. In his mind he had put *Alabama* together so he could sail the two boats in company, not to be left in the quarter wake. I tried to strike a balance between Bob's wishes and the crew's. Of course the crew was not as content sailing over to Cow Bay or Tarpaulin Cove week after week when they could make it to Newport, wind or no.

One week, I had decided to stay with Bob and sail in company with *Shenandoah*. During this week we put in to Cow Bay, just east of Oak Bluffs and west of Edgartown along the State Beach area of Martha's Vineyard. The following morning the wind was southwest, howling through the shrouds and rigging, but there was no sea under the lee of State Beach. I'd gone over to *Shenandoah* and had breakfast with Bob. We talked about different places we could go according to the forecast. One of the ideas was to stay there for the day and send the kids ashore to play on the beach. How it was suggested I'm not sure, but it turned out to be the best suggestion of all, and that was to get underway and go for a sail under the protection of State Beach.

We got underway, and sailed the vessels back and forth between Oak Bluffs and Edgartown until mid-afternoon. We had those two boats at times only a boat length from each other. Side by side the two vessels ranged along, one trying to outdo the other. *Alabama* is no match for *Shenandoah*, which has a longer waterline and a greater spread of canvas. While reaching back and forth I tried to stay to windward of *Shenandoah* and keep her in the dirty air off my aft quarter. As we got to the extremity of our racetrack Bob would signal with a wave in the air and start to head up, initiating his tack. In 'Bama I could come up into the wind and fall off on my new tack before Bob was full and by. I would gain some distance between us, but in a short minute or two *Shenandoah* would return to my quarter. She would range ahead under my lee, stall, and settle at my quarter again. It was so impressive to have these two boats so close together and see the power in *Shenandoah's* abilities.

Now I have done this with dinghies and in 50-foot yachts, but never big vessels. We threw those boats around like they were little dinghies playing in a pond. I've often wondered what it looked like from the beach, looking out over these two vessels playing this cat and mouse game. It was a glorious day of sailing nowhere with my friend Bob Douglas.

Alabama's only advantage against *Shenandoah* may be found in a full-blown race where she could make the windward mark in a quarter of the time *Shenandoah* would take. Whether 'Bama could hold on to the lead in the downwind leg or the reaching legs, I do not know.

"Hey, do you remember..."

OF ALL THE LINES ON THE SCHOONER, THE PEAK and throat have always been the hardest for me to handle. They are long, heavy and awkward. They consume a coil (600 feet) of 1-inch rope per mast, the peak using 375 feet and the throat using the remaining 225 feet.

The peak and throat halyards are free of exceptions; with regard to a block year, all of the keepers face to starboard on the peak and the shackle pins all go in from top down. On the throat, the keepers all face aft, because these blocks are up against the mast and the back sides of them are unseen. The hauling end should come off the forward sheave, with the keeper facing aft. With this tackle being led from the hauling end, it's rove in the forward sheave. If you reeve the line through the blocks with the blocks in the same attitude to each other, then the line will reeve through the third sheave or aftmost of the triple. This is where the jig would be shackled in place, and with the gear hanging in place, the jig will be on the starboard side in the aftmost sheave. The throat on the main and the fore have two little fairlead blocks each, one port and one to starboard, shackled to the futtock collar to pull the halyard away from the gaff jaws when the sail is set. On the jig side of this tackle, the halyard leads forward and hard over one of the cheeks of the block. This produces a chafe spot, but it's less important than the fairlead of the hauling end on the port side, which also shackles to the futtock collar leading the halyard forward, but not as hard over the cheek of the block.

In rigging the peak halyard, there are two single blocks on the gaff, a single at the masthead, and a double 4 feet below it on the mast. The hauling end comes from the deck on the starboard side and on the main goes aft of everything: from the crosstrees to the single at the masthead, where it is rove forward to aft, then down to the gaff and rove aft to forward in the aftmost block or peak end of the gaff. From here, the line goes back up the mast to the double and is rove through the port sheave aft to forward and then back to the forward block or throat end of the gaff and rove forward to aft. The last pass is back to the masthead and rove aft to forward through the starboard sheave of the double block. This is where the jig is attached, which goes off to the port rail. This double block may seem odd in that the jig does not hang from the sheave of the side the jig is on, but with the block rove in this way it twists and creates the least amount of friction on the cheeks of the block by the other parts of the tackle while the sail is set. The fore and main are set up with their peaks and throats in the same manner. The only difference is that with the fore, the peak halyard is rove through the crosstrees, whereas on the main it is aft of the crosstrees. This is because the trestle trees were lengthened many years ago to rake the topmast shrouds aft more and allow the yards to brace up more sharply.

The peak and throat halyards are the same length on the fore and the main. With *Shenandoah* using manila rope instead of synthetics, it is necessary to replace or end-for-end the running gear every so often. There has been a lot of flak about the use of the manila and the time spent in maintaining the running rigging, but I see it as a valuable lesson in maintenance and in the art of handling rope. These vessels claim to be school ships. The maintenance needs to be part of the lessons. It does not happen by itself, and in my opinion, if more maintenance was taught, then less major work and money would be needed in the long run of the vessel's career. I feel *Shenandoah* is a prime example of this. In her fifty years of service she has undergone less major work then the *Gamage,* a vessel built at the same yard and only a month earlier, but not maintained in the same way. In my time on the schooner, I have end-for- ended and replaced a good bit of *Shenandoah's* rope and some of the standing rig. Once or twice we've done these exercises underway. This adds a bit of complication to the job, which in some cases is hard enough. With the description of reeving off the peak halyard or the throat halyard, you can imagine the number of trips up and down the shrouds with a 1-inch diameter rope, total length of about 350 feet.

One of the tricks I learned, and how I came about this I don't remember, was to tie the bitter end of the halyard to one of the parts that travels to the masthead. This makes it possible for two men to reeve the halyard without making trips up and down the shrouds as they overhaul the halyard. The second trick was in end-for-ending the peak or the throat halyards. You start by joining the hauling end and the jig ends together. This can be done with a long splice or whippings and marryings. Then you can stand on the deck and haul the halyard through the blocks, creating a large circle. As you replace the peak of the main with the peak of the fore, you put the ends on the opposite sides of the vessel.

Now if the bo'sun has his act together, the peaks and throats are on a three-year schedule where the first year they're brand new. Second-year, now a season old, he will end-for-end them, and the third year finishes them off, They're replaced at the end of the season or in the beginning of the new season. Now end-for-ending means that the hauling end on deck is swapped with the jig end or dead end up aloft. This works because in many instances, there is a certain amount of rope from the bitter end of the hauling end that is never under strain because of distance up the mast, lengths on the deck, or any number of reasons, but this allows us to use that rope twice. This tying the ends together trick can't be used in too many places. The small boat's falls lend themselves to the idea the same way as do the peaks and throats, but that's about the extent of it. The yawl boat falls don't, primarily because the stern fall is so much longer than the bow fall but the end of the stern fall can make a bow fall. I always figured the peak and throat were enough. They are big pieces of gear and I've never been up for an entire day of climbing up and down shrouds.

Handling the peak or the throat on a good day is a task of its own. When it's not a block year, getting the peak and throat up in place is hard work. Fleeting these tackles, particularly the throat, is a nightmare. It so badly wants to be twisted that you spend more time keeping it untwisted than you do fleeting it out. With the peak, twists are less of a problem with all of the separate parts; instead, each pass of the peak halyard goes to a separate block so you end up with a tangled mess. But I'll never forget handling the peak halyard while sailing down Vineyard Sound.

I don't remember where we were bound, Cuttyhunk or Tarpaulin Cove, but it does not matter because it was a beautiful summer day, crystal clear with fifteen to eighteen knots of wind. Even though it was such a gentle easy sail, everyone was still watching the gear. Everyone keeps their eyes on the vessel for potential problems: the crew, Bob, and myself. Well, someone noticed that the main peak halyard had started to let go

Waiting for a chance along.

up at the masthead. One strand had parted and the two busted ends were flapping in the breeze. Bob wanted to strike the sail but I was afraid the bitter ends of the broken strands would get jammed up in the blocks and put a stop to getting the sail down, or back up. I proposed putting up a temporary halyard to take the strain off the gaff and sail, then end-for-ending the halyard. This approach would allow us ample time to either sail the schooner into a harbor of refuge, or to get lucky enough to finish the job underway. After some more thought and discussion Bob agreed to let us try it.

So with the task in hand, we set out to accomplish it. I say we, and I mean my crew and me. I have been very lucky when it comes to crew. They have always been very willing to help me get work done. With a dock line and a snatch block taken to the masthead, we fashioned a single-part peak halyard. It was a little hair-raising to walk the gaff while staring at that parted halyard, but there was no other way to tie the dock line around the gaff. Once this dock line was reeved off through the snatch block stropped to the masthead, we sent the bitter end to the deck. The dock line went about halfway down the mast, at which point we coupled it to a four-part tackle with a second four part tackle on the hauling part of the first tackle, and both of these tackles were anchored to the chain plates. With all set up, we took a strain and relieved the broken peak halyard of its duty. During the course of un-reeving the peak halyard and getting it back together the other way around, we had to take up once or twice on our temporary halyard because of stretch in the dock line.

I don't remember how long it took us, but we all worked with a will. It was about halfway through the season and everybody was pretty familiar with the schooner. The whole task was a great success; no one got hurt and nothing broke. In the Mattapoisett Inn that night there were drinks all around with embellished stories of our death-defying feats. Of course that story went on for a good couple weeks around the waterfront of Vineyard Haven, and every once in a while Bob brings it up, saying, "Hey, do you remember…." Over the years Captain Robert S. Douglas has been quite agreeable in letting me try things we both have read about. It has been really a pleasure to sail with him and play with his boat, and I can say many of those things we have all read about are true.

With the main and fore being the subject, let's look at the boom lifts. *Shenandoah's* main boom lifts are made up with two four-part tackles but the fore boom lifts are made up with only a single four-part tackle. The most notable detail with these lifts is the twist in them. This twist is so that when the gaff jaws meet the lower blocks of this tackle, the blocks roll off instead of hanging up on the jaws. If we were to use the centerline of the schooner as the reference point, then the sheaves of the block attached to the wire lift should be 90 degrees to the centerline, not parallel to it. The blocks shackled to the trestletrees have their sheaves in line with the centerline. That puts the keeper facing outboard whereas the lower block's keepers face aft. When rigging the lower blocks, the shackles should be outboard to inboard with the pin, and the top block should have the becket inboard so that the hauling end will reeve off the inboard sheave, which helps to twist the tackle. Once we leave the four-part tackle at the trestletrees and go for the deck, the main and fore do two different things. The fore goes down to the third pin in from forward on the fore pin rail on both port and starboard, but the main is shackled onto a second four-part tackle. There is nothing special about this second purchase. Its bottom block shackles to the eye bolts in the rail and its hauling ends go to, now, the second from last pin in the main pin rail, port and starboard. When *Shenandoah* was re-topped in Maine, the main pin rail was extended by one more belaying pin. This was done so the pin rail could be bolted to the stanchions. With fewer stanchions in *Shenandoah's* waist, the aft pin rail worked out to have an extra pin in it.

Bringing up the Rear

THE YAWL BOAT IS AN APPROPRIATE SUBJECT to end this book with, for she has always brought up the rear. The yawl boat was built by Arno Day, but her designer is a little unclear. Havilia Hawkin's yawl boat for *Mary Day* seems to have been a starting point for the design.

Every summer, the crew talk would include a segment about the yawl and how important she is. Bob would say, "It's like the family car." A statement so alien to our youth. "We all need to keep track of 'er and take care of her. Without 'er, none of us will be going anywhere." Despite Bob's vigilance, that poor little boat has been hard used once or twice over the years. Actually, the yawl boat I came to know and love came to an untimely end in the middle of July 2015, while safe in her place high up on the davits astern of *Shenandoah*.

Put me in! I'm ready.

Bob had *Shenandoah* anchored up to the northwest of old number "6"N in Vineyard Haven Harbor when the yawl was the recipient of an ill-fated mariner's misjudgment. She was old and fragile after fifty-one years of hard use. She did not withstand the accident, and passed on.

As I have mentioned, *Shenandoah*, 170 tons of vessel, has no auxiliary power. No engine except what was in that little 16 foot long 6 foot wide yawl boat that hangs on the stern davits. Her power came from an old four-cylinder Ford diesel of 58 horsepower, with an Osco conversion to make it marine

usable. Now, it's a Volvo Penta with 120 horsepower, in a boat begun by Elmer Colimer and finished off by Miles Therlow. Every morning, whether in the water or out, the bo'sun checks the oil, coolant, fuel, belts, starter, lamps and flashlights. He is responsible for the little boat's condition and every two weeks he changes the oil and filter.

All 2,800 pounds of the yawl hangs from the davits by two tackle, made up from two 3/4-inch triples and two 3/4-inch doubles with hooks. These boat falls are mirror images of each other. The keepers on the top blocks face outboard and forward on the bottom blocks. The hooks should be open to the same side as the keeper, so it should be forward also. When the boat is in the water and the falls are slacked, the blocks lay down so the hooks can just be picked up off the eyebolts. The hauling end should come out of the center of the top triple block.

Now these falls are put together with a twist, meaning the top and bottom blocks are 90 degrees to each other. This can create some confusion if you don't see how the line is rove through the blocks. If we take the bow fall and stand in front of it so our perspective is looking aft, then the reeving is as follows:

From the hauling end in the center of the triple block, down to the aft sheave of the double and inside to outside of this sheave. Up to the triple, aft to forward of the outboard sheave. Down to the forward sheave of the double and overboard to inboard, then up to the triple's inside sheave. Forward to aft on this inside sheave of the triple, and down to be spliced on the aft side of the becket for the double.

Now, this last pass puts a cross over the first pass, but there's nothing you can do about it. You can change the order, so the first pass goes from outside to inside, but the last turn will still cross. There is no becket on the double, so that this tackle, when two-blocked, comes together tight.

With *Shenandoah's* most recent re-topping, the stern has been altered so that the falls no longer have to be in their most aft position on the davits but can be in the forward position. Also, the falls no longer need to be two-blocked like they did prior to the re-topping. The bow fall is still two-blocked, but the stern fall is left with a space the size of a block between the two blocks.

The stern fall is a mirror image of the bow fall. If it's a block year, the only difference is the stern fall is a longer piece of line than the bow fall. *Shenandoah* pushes with the yawl boat tucked up under the starboard side. Many times the boat is dropped and left hooked up to the falls for speed or safety. Consequently, the stern fall gets fleeted out to a fairly long distance. The stern fall should be long enough so that when the yawl boat is in reverse the hauling end on deck still stretches to the forward end of the main house. Of course, with the bow fall the line does not need to be as long, but with the yawl boat in reverse, the hauling end should still reach the forward end of the main house. This distance is adequate for about ten people to line the side deck and pull on the falls, although we the crew have managed to get the boat up with just the six of us, seven if you include the mate. Once the boat is halfway raised we'd go from side to side to get it all the way out.

Bob has, for all the years I've known him, coiled these two lines into two small coils not to exceed three deck planks in diameter. He will redo what someone else has done if it is not a neat, small coil. I have never gotten a clear answer to why, but I guess it's just his will. One thing he did say one time was "They make good coils to toss to a man overboard." Although these coils do hang from the davits over the cleats of the main sheet, if they were done too long, they would interfere with the handling of it.

One time at the end of a season, we didn't get the boat hauled out and put in the shed in time for a bad gale. There were only three of us downrigging the schooner, and Bob was worried about the yawl boat. So we lifted it out on the davits by running the falls forward to the capstan. It was slow, but effective.

Day sails were canceled if we did not get fourteen people. Bob would say we needed seven per fall to lift the boat. Bill for some reason always would sing Whiskey Johnny to lift the yawl.

Whiskey is the life of man Whiskey O! Johnny O!
O, whiskey is the life of man Whiskey for my Johnny O!

O, I drink whiskey when I can Whiskey from an old tin can

Whiskey gave me a broken nose! Whiskey made me pawn my clothes

Whiskey drove me around Cape Horn It was many a month when I was gone

I thought I heard the old man say:
I'll treat my crew in a decent way

A glass of grog for every man! And a bottle for the shanty Man

When I started on *Shenandoah,* the yawl boat would hit the water as soon as sail was stowed. The first run into shore was always with the trash and to get ice for the deck box, unless we were in Tarps. If we had come in with the yawl boat pushing, then she would stay in the water unless the weather was to become bad overnight.

Pushing is done with the little boat tucked up under the starboard counter, running in forward at about half throttle. With the yawl boat in this line of work, there needs to be less than 15 knots of wind and calm seas. The yawl boat cannot push the schooner in anything more than 18 knots of wind. There are a set of hand signals Bob uses to control the boat and signal to the bo'sun what he wants (see appendix).

The boat's bow is tied with three lines. The first is the centerline, the main tow line, which goes from the bow of the yawl boat up and over the rail.

It's made on the cleat next to the wheelbox to starboard. The other two lines act as spring lines to prevent the bow of the yawl boat from slipping out from under the counter port or starboard. They lead from the bow of the yawl to the aft corners of the schooner where the davit braces land on the rail port and starboard. If reverse is ever needed the bo'sun will toss up the stern line and Bob will make it on the port davit brace. The

Pushing.

bo'sun, who is in command of the little boat while pushing, was not allowed forward of the main mast or out of Bob's sight generally while we were pushing. It is the bo'sun's job to keep an eye on the gauges and operate the gear box and throttle. The yawl boat is always ready for action, no matter if hauled out on her davits or not.

I heard one time Bob was pushing in Vineyard Sound when a good-sized power boat went by, throwing a huge wake. The bo'sun, who was hanging out on deck, did not get in the boat fast enough to stop the yawl from being "drowned." This means the stern of the schooner pushes the bow of the yawl boat underwater as the schooner pitches due to the wave. To prevent this, the bo'sun throws the yawl boat into reverse and keeps her out from under the schooner's counter until the sea calms down.

On this occasion, the bo'sun managed to save the yawl boat, I'm told. He got her out from under the counter for the second dip. Luckily the first dip did not flood the engine, which runs the bilge pump.

A friend of mine relayed a story to me about almost sinking the yawl boat while in the Mystic River. Bob and *Shenandoah* were going up the Mystic River under sail with a breeze that was slowly letting go. Bob decided to drop the yawl boat in and push the rest of the way to the Seaport. The yawl boat needs two people to lower her into the water, one on the bow fall and one on the stern fall, and you always hold one turn on the cleats. For this occasion, a young, overly helpful fellow took up the stern fall without any concept of the weight he was handling. He undid the stern fall from the cleat and the weight of the boat tore the rope through his hands. With the stern fall free and the bow fall not, the yawl boat was hanging from its davits, stern down, across the stern of the schooner. Apparently they were able to lift the stern of the yawl back out before the boat filled with too much water.

All of this was happening while the schooner was sailing up the Mystic River, mind you. It must've been a hectic experience for Bob and his mate, having a sixteen-foot-long bucket dragging astern. As I write, it has just come to me why Bob for all these years I've known him, has always handled the stern fall when lowering the boat into the water. Ideally, the boat is slacked into the water parallel to the water because of how the little boat is tied up to the schooner for pushing. The bow could never fall so that it would go underwater. The main tow line when pushing prevents the yawl boat's bow from going underwater. Actually, we try to tie the bow slightly hanging on the main towline. This takes into consideration any stretching the rope may have if we are pushing hard. This day and this experience must be why for all the years I've known Bob he has been the only one, unless not on board, to lower or handle the stern fall when getting the boat launched.

I'll relay one more story about the little yawl boat and *Shenandoah*, then I'll leave their trials and tribulations to the annals of history and those of us who were there. While in Padanaram Harbor on a week cruise, the yawl was in the employ of passenger trips to and from the town landing. While she was on her way on this fine evening, she got tangled up with some rocks. Bob and I had retired to our quarters for the night. After a short time Bob woke me from my doghouse to say, "The yawl boat has been stove in on some rocks near the yacht club and sunk. I'm going ashore in a Whitehall to see."

In my early years on *Shenandoah*, Bob and his schooner were catering to adults, most of whom wanted and needed the attractions the "beach" provided. I have always termed anything ashore as "on the beach." To me, it meant I was aground and stuck; to be on the beach or to have to deal with aspects of it was not my thing. The yawl boat would run folks to and from the beach all night. Invariably this went on 'til one in the morning because a large group would wait for the "last boat" at midnight, making for too many people for one trip in the yawl boat.

Padanaram is a harbor that requires an hour round trip, schooner to beach and back. It's the practice during the day to run through the mooring field to shorten the trip; not by much, mind you. In Padanaram, the boatman can judge his water during the day but it's best to stay in the channel at night. The mooring field on the eastern shore is shallow and rocky.

When Bob got to the little boat he found her tied up alongside the yacht club dock so that the rail was awash. It is very important to give the boatman some credit for getting the yawl boat to the nearest dock and preventing a diving job. With the help of the Padanaram harbormaster, they got the yawl boat tied alongside the harbormaster's boat and towed out to *Shenandoah*, where we lifted the yawl boat on her davits and assess the damage.

With the yawl boat on her davits and safe from any more harm, Bob called up Charlie Mitchell and asked him to tow us around into New Bedford. It must have been around eleven or twelve o'clock at night when this all happened. I remember the talk on the radio; Charlie was upset over the hour. It's funny to think about this now. We called Charlie at home on his phone but from the schooner's VHF. For you kids reading this, we had a marine operator that patched a VHF radio through to a landline telephone. No cell phones in those days. Hard to believe that much time has passed and I'm getting old enough to say things like that. Bob was insistent on the move for fear of the wind coming up and him not having his yawl boat. Charlie came with his tug, *Jaguar*, around one in the morning to tow us. He positioned us on the north side of Old Wharf, Fairhaven, where we spent the rest of the night.

Come morning, Charlie came back with *Jaguar* and we lowered the yawl boat from the davits onto the stern of Jaguar's working deck. Bob and Charlie went in to Kelly's Shipyard where, with the yard travel lift, they lifted the yawl boat up off *Jaguar's* deck and took it ashore. In those days Kelly's Shipyard still had a carpenter; old Louis was his name. He was a little man with thick glasses and a worn-out painter's hat. He talked with a very strong Portuguese accent and waddled more than walked. The old man took about a day to fix up the little boat. I remember the old man never used a ruler but always had a stick to mark measurements with. He put two new short planks down by the garboard with butt blocks. I remember him giving Bob a hard time about the frames in the little boat. He would say, "Bob dese frames no good, dey like cheese. Nuttin for dey screw to grab."

That weekend Bob was changing the oil in the yawl boat and happened to see in the bilge. Old Louis had put all the screws in alongside the frames. The only fastenings holding the planks in place were on the two ends with the butt blocks. Bob was not very happy, and come next time the boat was on the davits, Bob added screws where they were supposed to be.

From Kelly's Shipyard, the yawl boat went back into the water and *Shenandoah* resumed her week cruise. We lost two days dealing with the yawl boat and had some upset passengers. But it all turned out okay in the end; really, it was minor. "Nobody drownded. Fact, nothing to laugh at at all." (Marriott Edgar).

So many folks get all upset over mistakes or accidents that are really minor. I try to remember the old adages like: "The price of freedom is eternal vigilance," (Jefferson); "What can't be 'elped must be endured; every cloud 'as a silvery lining," (Marriott Edgar); and "Few plans withstand contact with the enemy," (Von Moltke). Three of my best friends are always using these quotes when things are going afoul.

We all have made mistakes or misjudgments. Some of them attract a large audience; some are never noticed. Some of us are gracious in our misfortunes, and some are not. It all adds to our experience and builds our character. What separates the leaders from the followers is how we use that experience. Some people become great teachers and help others, and some people use their experience as a tool against their fellow man. Then there are those who never learn to use it either way and continue to fumble along. This has been some of my experience; good, bad, and indifferent. I have done my part in sharing it with you. Now it is up to you to do with it what you can. May your anchors never foul.

Leave her, Johnny

Oh the times was hard and the wages low
Leave her, Johnny, leave her

And the grub was bad and the gales did blow
And it's time for me to leave her

Leave her, Johnny, leave her

Oh, leave her, Johnny, leave her

For the voyage is done and the winds do blow

And it's time for me to leave her

I thought I heard the Old Man say
You can go ashore and take your pay
Oh her stern was foul and the voyage was long
The winds was bad and the gales was strong
And I'll leave her tight and I'll leave her trim
And heave the hungry packet in
Oh, leave her, Johnny, leave her with a grin
For there's many a worser I've sailed in
And now it's time to say goodbye
For the old pierhead's a-drawing nigh.

Appendix

Crew Through the Years

Mate:	Bo'sun:	Cook:
1964 Tony Higgins	Bill Bunting	Dan Goodenough
65 Tony Higgins	Terry Townsend	Hugh Johnson
66 George Adams	Matthew Stackpole	Dan Goodenough
67 George Adams	Matthew Stackpole	Joe Momola
68 Matthew Stackpole	Tom Reynolds (midseason shift)	
69 Matthew Stackpole	Tom Reynolds	Dick O'Connell
70 Matthew Stackpole	Tom Reynolds	Dick O'Connell
1970 Matthew Stackpole	Tom Reynolds	Dick O'Connell
71 Tom Reynolds	Roger Hathaway	Dick O'Connell
72 Tom Reynolds	Roger Hathaway	Charlie Leighton
73 Tom Reynolds	Bill Austin	David Poppe
74 Bill Austin	Scott Young	Bruce Fisher
75 Scott Young	Bill Mabie	Bruce Fisher
76 Scott Young	Bill Mabie	Steve Souci "Sooch"
77 Bill Mabie		Steve Souci
78 Bill Mabie	Jon Lange	Steve Souci
79 Bill Mabie	Jon Lange	Joey Hall
1980 Bill Mabie	Carl Fry	Joey Hall
81 Bill Austin	Gary Maynard	John Anderson
82 Bill Austin	Gary Maynard	John Anderson
83 Bob Leitch	Charlie Belden	Barbara Knudsen
84 Charlie Belden	Andrew Miller	Barbara Knudsen
85 Charlie Belden	Andrew Miller	Marshall Jett
86 Gary Maynard	Chris LaPointe	Marshall Jett
87 Chris LaPointe*	Mike Robinson	Marshall Jett
88 Chris LaPointe	Robbie Douglas	Joe Keenan
89 Geoff Jones	Doug Randall	Joe Keenan
1990 Troy Canham	Dominic Zachorne (midseason shift)	Joe Keenan
91 Jeff Thompson	Dominic Zachorne (midseason shift)	Steve Baracus
	Filled in when Steve left	Rick Hamilton
		NormaJean "Mike" Zachorne
92 Jeff Thompson	Dominic Zachorne	Joe Keenan
93 Dominic Zachorne		Stacey
94 Dominic Zachorne	Jamie Douglas	Tanya Koch
95 Jamie Douglas	Morgan Douglas	Tanya Koch
96 Jamie Douglas	Morgan Douglas	Andy Jackson
97 Morgan Douglas	Dan Nelson	Jim Puff
98 Morgan Douglas	Matt Cabral	Jim Puff
99 Morgan Douglas	Matt Cabral	Jim Puff
2000 Dominic Zachorne	Brooke Douglas	Jim Puff
01 Morgan Douglas	Brooke Douglas	Jim Puff
02 Ian Ridgeway	Ben Slotten	Jim Puff
03 Ian Ridgeway	Brad Woodworth	David Olearceck
04 Ian Ridgeway	Brad Woodworth	Brian Fiske

05	Ian Ridgeway	Brad Woodworth	Brian Fiske
06	Brad Woodworth	Todd Woodworth	Joe Keenan
07	Todd Woodworth	Declan Frey	Phil Keenan
08	Todd Woodworth	Declan Frey	Ryan Dickerson
09	Todd Woodworth	Kevin Black	Dave Keenan
2010	Josh Ingersol	Bob Sengstacken	Phil Keenan
11	Bob Sengstacken	Duffy Sobella	Mary Ellen Muziel
12	Bob Sengstacken	Chris O'Riley	Megan D'Olimpio
13	Bob Sengstacken	Chris O'Riley	Nick Clanton
14	Robert "Bear" Harding***	Andrew Ducy	Nick Clanton
		Mike DeGiovanna (mid-season shift)	
15	Robert "Bear" Harding	Alex Troxel	Nick Clanton
		Eric Jederlinik (mid-season shift)	
16	Robert "Bear" Harding	Will Livingston	Nick Clanton
17	Robert "Bear" Harding	William "Sam" Shields	Phillip Keenan
18	William "Sam" Shields	Chase Garretson	Sheri Sullivan

Patte Kane   Patty Kelly   Jessy Sterges   Fox   Katy Parker

Trivia

One keg of nails per strake, thirty strakes per side.

Bill Rise did all the joinery work on the schooner at the Gamage yard.

Bill marred Harvey's daughter.

Harvey passed away in 1976 at seventy-six years old.

Eddy Gamage was the head of the iron working department and made all the iron work for the schooner.

Steering gear is an oscillating No.9, patented February 24, 1874, and bought for fifty dollars from the Morse yard in Thomaston.

The capstan came from Bath Iron Works.

In the last sea chanty "Leave Her, Johnny," I changed the word "us" to "me" and "we" to "I."

Charlie Sayles made the quarterboards for *Shenandoah*.

Books of Interest

Masting & Rigging: The Clipper Ship & Ocean Carrier, Harold A. Underhill.
Young Sea Officer's Sheet Anchor, Darcy Lever Esq.
The Sailor's Word Book, Admiral W. H. Smyth
The Marlinspike Sailor, Hervey G. Smith.
American Fishing Schooners, Howard I. Chapelle.
Eagle Seamanship - A Manual for Square-Rigger Sailing, United States Naval Institute, Annapolis, Maryland

Dead-eye lanyards

The tightening down of the dead-eye lanyards has been something many have asked me about. I have never done anything special with regards to tightening them. On *Shenandoah* to tighten down the lower shrouds, I have always used the throat halyards and jigs on the bitter end of the lanyard. On the second pass of the lanyard I have used a four-part tackle. This I have found to work well in rendering the looseness through the lanyard. If I have two crew, one outboard and one inboard, swaying on the lanyards, somebody else or myself will tighten up on the tackles. I have never used grease on the deadeyes because *Shenandoah* has always catered to passengers and I've tried to keep the deck free of sticky, gooey things that people can get into. With two tackle on the dead-eye lanyards, grease has never been a necessity. I can actually wring a mast and make the dead-eye lanyards tighter than they ought to be.

With regards to tension for the lanyards, I have always grabbed the lanyards in their center, meaning halfway between each dead-eye, and squeezed them together. I have tried for a tension that does not allow the lanyard to flex more than a quarter of the overall diameter of the lanyards, but not less than the diameter of the lanyard's rope.

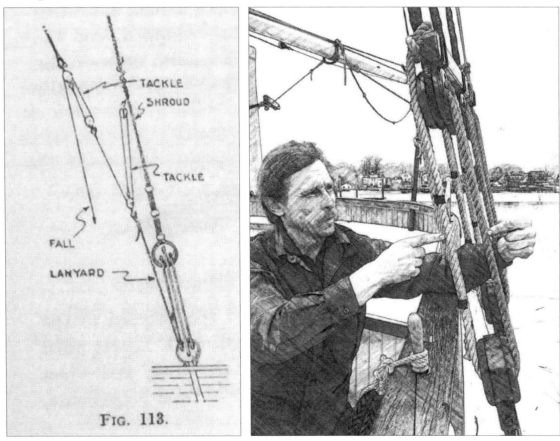

Photo of the author describing tension of the dead eyes.
(Photo by David Eusa)

Yawl Boat Hand Signals

If Bob puts his hand in alignment with the schooner's center line, pointing aft, he wants the yawl straight astern.

Bob will point to port when he wants the yawl's stern kicked over to port.

Bob will point to starboard when he wants the yawl's stern kicked to starboard.

A flat hand from Bob could mean two things. If he pats the air as if he were patting the head of a dog, then he is looking to slow down. If he swings his hand out and back in a level plan, then he wants neutral in the gearbox.

This hand signal is a tough one to show. What Bob is doing is turning his finger in the air. He will either turn it toward him, which means more power out of the gearbox, or turn it toward you in the yawl boat. That means he wants reverse and he will continue to turn his hand until you give him the power he wants, and you'll see a fist. We all know that means "hold that."

These two fingers locked together mean he wants you to "hook her up," meaning to fleet the falls and hook them on the yawl in preparation for hauling the boat out. The yawl boat is usually in neutral at this point, being dragged by its tow line.

Tacking *Shenandoah*

This may seem odd to write down but it is part of the documentation of what we did. As with many boats tacking *Shenandoah* has lessons to be learned. For example, in a big sea, the sea can hold her from coming up on the wind, slowing her momentum and making her miss stays. Without the tops'l on, we used a "tacking tackle" on the main boom to draw the mains'l to windward. This would help force her around by kicking her stern to leeward.

Without the tops'l on, Bob would put his hand in the air and turn his finger in a circular motion. If no one was watching him he would yell out "abou'". Then the mate would yell out "tack'n". One crew would go aft and help on the tacking tackle if Bob had not coerced one of the passengers to help. The mate takes a position on the lee side to let go of the sheets once *Shenandoah* is clear of stays and the head sails can be passed. The crew take up the sheets in readiness to receive the head sails as they're passed. Bob puts the helm down and *Shenandoah* answers the command. On the foredeck, the heads'ls thunder if there is a good breeze on. She comes to the wind and the heads'ls press against the stays. She starts to fall off. Bob holds the heads'ls until there is no longer a luff in the main's luff. Once he sees that, he will either point with his finger to leeward, or if you're not paying attention, he will yell out "g' ead." If it's a hard breeze and she is falling off fast, he will let go of the heads'ls sooner. This helps the crew because, loaded with a wind, the jibs are heavy. When there is a good breeze and we are asked to trim a heads'l, it takes four on the rail and one to tail. With the head sails sheeted in and the schooner full and by, the crew go aft to the braces. The mate takes the windward side to slack out and the crew to leeward to haul in. Bracing up without the tops'ls on helps to reduce windage aloft.

With the tops'ls set, the tacking tackle is not needed and when the heads'ls are handled differently. Once she is on the wind the tops'l is very much aback, and there is no way of her missing stays. The head sails are not pressed against the stays but can be passed. Many times the crew oversheet in this tack because hauling in is so easy. Sometimes, if the wind is real light, Bob will wait to pass the head sails, just to give that extra kick in falling off on her new tack. With the tops'ls set the crew do not just brace up, but wait for Bob to yell out "g' ead." He likes to keep the squares aback till she is full and by, then he braces up on the new tack.

To be "full an' by" for Bob, means to have the main gaff in alignment with the colors at the masthead. Bob uses the colors as his windvane, and in going to windward, Shenandoah can split 110 degrees.

Stowing the topsail on *Shenandoah*

Four crew head aloft, one at the end of the yoke arm in the center of the yard and one by the second buntline fairlead on the yard, port and starboard. Someone on deck let's go of the buntl'ns and leachl'ns, allowing the sail to drop from its gear and hang from the yard. Once the sail is dropped from the gear, you need to find the foot of the sail, more specifically, the leather chafing on the bolt rope. The two crew in the center of the yard take the foot with the leather on it and center it between themselves. Then, what I do is take the bolt rope of the leach from starboard or port, one or the other, and pass it to the opposite side. This is repeated on the other side. This makes a bight at the leather chafing on the bolt rope. This also makes the sail hang like a great triangle from the yard. Then I take and make another two similar flakes, each one makes a flake of canvas from the yard arm back to the center of the yard. This folds the sail on the yard as opposed to bunching. The more folding or flaking of the sail, the more likely the sail will be a smooth stow. Once the sail has been flaked, all four crew find the skin and proceed to roll the skin over the flaked sail or as we say, "dump". We created a bag, if you will, using the portion of the sail from jackstay to three feet out. This bag is hanging down on the front side of the yard and needs to be "busted up" onto the top of the yard. This is a heavy job, and all four crew need to work together. We first "beat" the bag against the yard, which allows or settles the sail into place. We then roll the bag up the face of the yard and onto the top. Once the sail is on the yard, wrinkles are worked out of the skin and the "ears" are made even port and starboard. At this point, the gaskets are wrapped around yard and sail. The "ears" are the clews of the sail stretched from the clewl'n blocks up and around the sail into the stow.

Jib stowing on *Shenandoah*

Stowing of the jibs is similar in that they are flaked down and then skinned over. With the sail down, one finds the miter flake. The flake is pulled out and held to the side of the downhaul block, as well as the flake above and below. All the rest of the sail is then worked to the opposite side. Enough of the miter is left out to form the skin. Starting with the head leach of the sail, one flakes it down on the miter flake. Flakes are made by drawing the sail aft along the bolt rope. Once all the leach is flaked, then start again at the clew and work along the boltrope of the foot. Flakes are set on top of what has already been set down. With leach and foot of the jib flaked, one now takes the folds of sail between each jib hank and rolls them into the head of the sail. Then the skin is pulled up and over the flakes to create a "sail cover" appearance. The miter should be on top down the center of the stow. At the head, the head and first flake are draped, port and starboard, to cover the top of the stow. The tack and first flake are pulled out from the opposite side of the downhaul and draped over the stay and jib hanks, also to cover the top of the stow. These last parts are arranged so rainwater will shed off the stow. Lastly, the sail is gasketed, and all wrinkles are worked out of the skin.

Glossary

Aback - A sail is aback when the wind strikes it on the forward side; this can be intentional in maneuvering or unexpected in a sudden wind shift.

Abeam - A direction away from either side of a vessel (90 degrees relative to the ship's heading).

Amidships - The portion of the vessel midway between the bow and stern or midway between the port and starboard sides.

Athwart - The transverse direction; anything that crosses the center line of a vessel.

Astern - A direction behind a vessel (180 degrees relative to the ship's heading).

Backstay - Standing rigging leading from a point on the mast to the rail abaft the mast.

Barque - A sailing vessel with three or more masts whose after mast is fore-and-aft rigged.

Barquentine - A sailing vessel with three or more masts whose foremast is square-rigged and after masts are rigged fore and aft.

Belay - Secure a line to a belaying pin, cleat, or other point established for this purpose.

Bend - 1) To fasten a sail securely to the jackstay on a yard, mast hoops, or hanks by means of robands.
   2) A method of fastening one line to another.

Bobstay - A heavy stay running from the stem of the ship to the end of the bowsprit.

Boltrope - Roping sown around the edges of a sail.

Bowsprit - The spar that extends out of the bow of a vessel.

Braces - Lines used to move the yards from one tack to another in a horizontal plane.

Buntl'ns - Buntlines - Lines used to douse a square sail's foot and bunt or body.

Cap Iron - An iron band at a masthead or bowsprit end to receive another spar.

Cheek Blocks - Blocks attached to the side of a yard at the outermost point to run square sail sheets through.

Clew - The corner of a sail made by foot and leech.

Clewl'n - Clewline - A line used to control the clew of a sail while dousing.

Close-hauled - Point of sail where a vessel is sailing as near to the wind as possible.

Club-hauling - The act of turning or tacking a vessel with an anchor.

Cockbill - Yards are cockbilled when they are canted out of horizontal.

Course - Lowest yard on a mast.

Cringle - Ring or grommet worked into the tabling of a sail at the head, clew, or leech. Used for making a line to.

Crosstree - Certain timbers that lay athwart ships at the upper ends of the mast to extend the spread of the topmast's shrouds.

Downhaul - A line tied at the head of a jib and led down the luff to a fairlead at the tack then back to the deck. Used to douse a sail.

Earring - The cringle in the corner of a square sail made by head and leech.

Ease - To pay out a line slowly.

End-for-end - To take a line, halyard, sheet, or otherwise and turn it so the dead end becomes the bitter end and bitter end becomes the dead end.

Fairlead - A block or fitting used to change the lead of a line.

Falls - The tackle used to launch or haul the small boats.

Fall Off - When a vessel changes course in a direction away from the wind.

Fid - A square block of wood to act as a key in the bottom end of a topmast to lock it into a hoisted position. Also a spike made of wood and used for splicing rope.

Fife Rail - A rail around three sides of a mast attached to the deck that running rigging from said mast is led to and belayed.

Fleet Out - To separate two blocks of a tackle and drawing the tackle to its extreme length. The opposite of "two-blocked."

Flemish Horse - A foot rope from yard out to yardarm end.

Foot - The bottom edge of a sail.

Footrope - A rope slung under a yard to provide a footing for the crew to work the sail of the yard.

Full and By - A point at which a vessel's sails are full of wind and the vessel is making way.

Futtock Shrouds - Iron rods between futtock band and crosstrees to provide a foundation for the topmast shrouds.

Gaff - The top spar of a four-sided fore-and-aft sail.

Gantline - A whip rigged aloft for general utility purposes.

Gasket - A line used to secure a sail or piece of gear.

Gripe - Lines or canvas straps used to secure a boat in its davits.

Halyard - Line or tackle used for hoisting and lowering sails and yards.

Head - Means many things, but here the top edge of a square sail and top edge of a fore-and-aft sail. Also the top corner of a jib headed sail.

Header - A temporary shift in the wind direction requiring a vessel to fall off.

Heave To - A maneuver done with a sailing vessel to stop or slow the vessel's headway and hold a position while at sea.

House, To - The act of lowering a topmast or retracting a jib boom.

In Irons - The act of a vessel missing stays or being poorly steered so that the vessel loses way and becomes unmanageable.

In its Gear - When a sail has been struck and is held by its buntlines, leechlines, clewlines or downhauls.

In its Lifts - When a yard is not being supported by its halyard but by its lifts. Also when a fore-and-aft sails boom is not supported by the sail but by its topping lift.

Jackline - A line to take the lowest mast hoops on a fore-and-aft sail or lowest hanks on a stay sail.

Jackstay - A wire or rope on a yard strung from yardarm base to yardarm base to bend the sail to.

Jib Boom - A spar extending out from the top of the bowsprit to extend the sail plan of a vessel.

Jig - A tackle added to, the dead end generally, of a halyard for added power.
>   Throat Jig, Peak Jig, Staysail Jig.

Leech - The aft side of a fore-and-aft sail, also the lee side edge of a square sail.

Leechline - leechl'n - A line used to control the leech of a square sail when dousing.

Leeway - Drift of a vessel perpendicular to her centerline.

Leeward - A direction downwind of; the vessel, the buoy, the headland.

Lifts - Wire pendants to support the yards or booms when not in use.

Line - Generally term given to rope on a vessel.

Luff - The weather edge of a sail. Also the motion sail makes when not full and by.

Marry - To join to lines by seizing or binding.

Martingale Stay - Wire or chain leading from dolphin striker to vessel port and starboard.

Miter - A multilayered panel off cloth in a jib or stay sail running from clew to luff and perpendicular to the luff.

Nock - A hollow cut out in the luff of the gaff topsail to form a better setting sail at the doublings.

Overhaul - Action of crew to slacken by hauling in the opposite direction to that in which the rope was drawn taut.

Pinch - To point too close to the wind so that the vessel does not have ample power to drive her.

Purchase - A general term for mechanical arrangement of blocks and line.

Quarter - A position 45 degrees abaft or ahead of the beam of a vessel; forward quarter, aft quarter.

Ringl'n - Ringline - A line used to handle the tack and bunt of a gaff top sail.

Robands - Lengths of twine or marline used to secure sails to mast hoops, hanks, or jackstays.

Running Rigging - All lines, ropes, blocks, wire, and gear used to make a sailing vessel function.

Seize - To fasten ropes, lines, or wire together using marline or small twine.

Sheet - Lines used to control the sail trim.

Slop Chest - A sea chest or large box on board a vessel full of items the crew may need. Shirts, pants, tobacco, boots, foul weather gear, and other personal things.

Standing Part - The fixed part of any piece of running rigging.

Stopper - A short length of line fixed to the deck, used to hold a halyard while the halyard is being belayed.

Strong Back - A timber that spans from the top of the port windlass bit to the top of the starboard windless bit.

Used to sling the anchor chain when not in use.

Strop - A line used to attach a tackle or bit of gear to; a shroud, a yard, a mast.

Sway, To - (NOT "To Sweat") The act of putting a strain on a line by a member of the crew to haul in slack.

Tack - The corner of a sail made by luff and foot.

Tacking - To bring a vessel into the wind and pass the wind from one side of the vessel to the other.

Trim Her - To adjust the sails of a vessel.

Two-blocked - Chock a-block - To draw the blocks of a tackle together so as to jam them against themselves.

Up Behind - Term used to let all who were hauling on a line know that the line has been secured and they can let go of the line.

Waist - The part of the vessel from deck to rail and stem to stern.

Wearing - The act of turning a vessel away from the wind and passing the wind from one side of the vessel to the other across her stern.

Weather, To - Upwind of (the buoy, the headland, the channel, the vessel).

Wring a Mast - Bend, cripple, or strain out of its natural position by setting shrouds up too taut.

Yard - A spar hung on a mast in a horizontal plan with equal lengths, port and starboard.

Yardarm - The outer end of a yard, port and starboard, not utilized for the sail.

Yoke - A wooden batten in the center of the yard for the yard to ride on the mast.

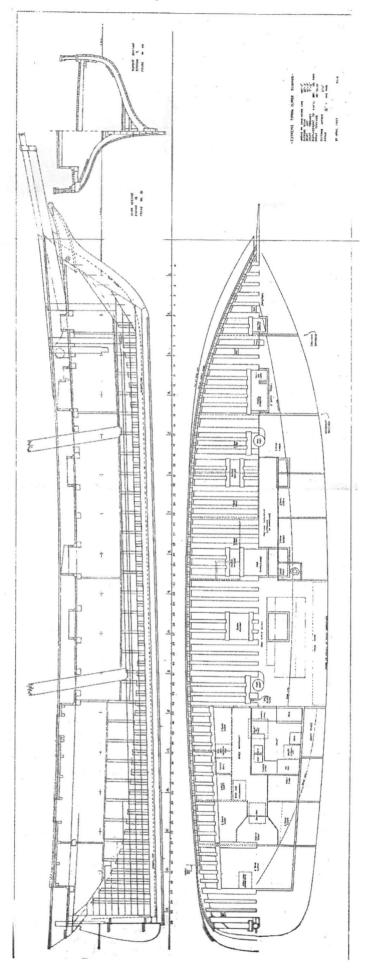

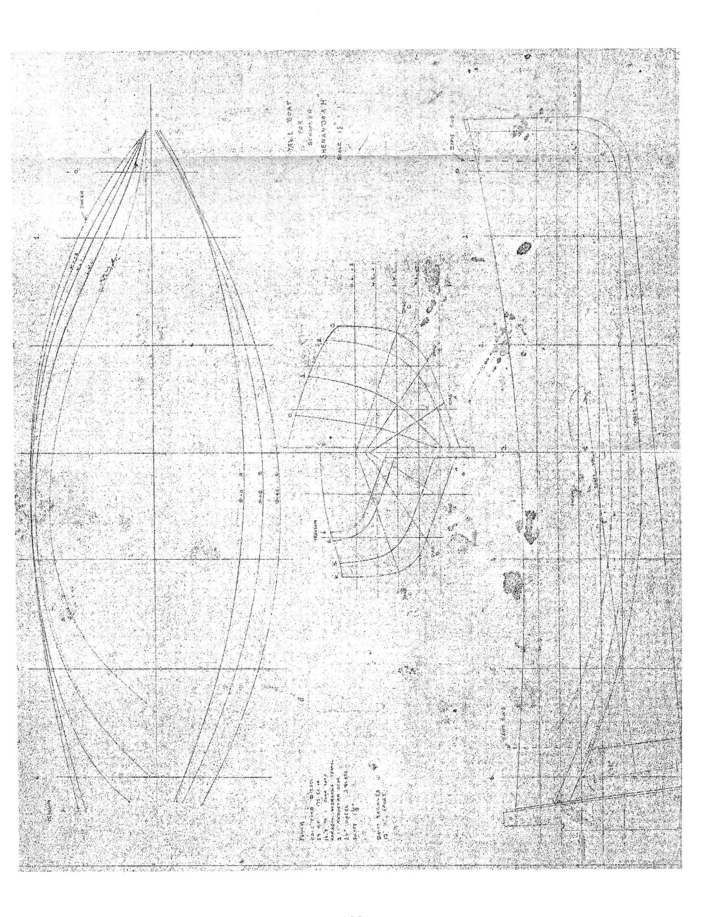

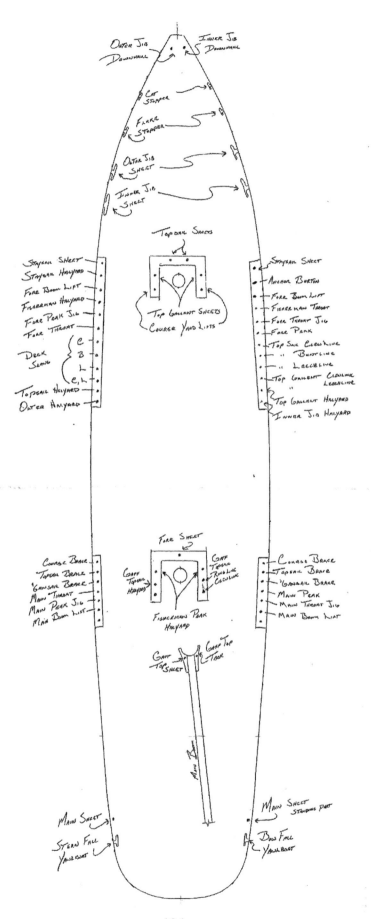

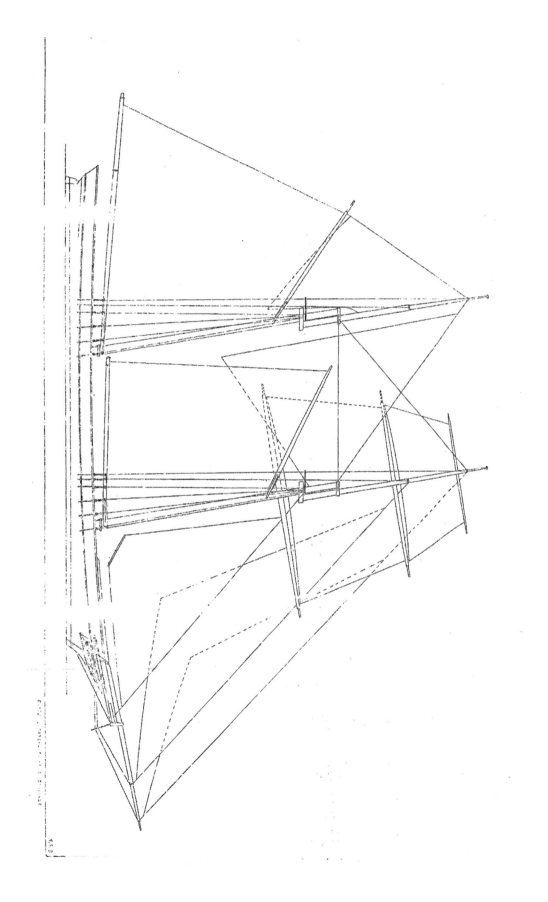

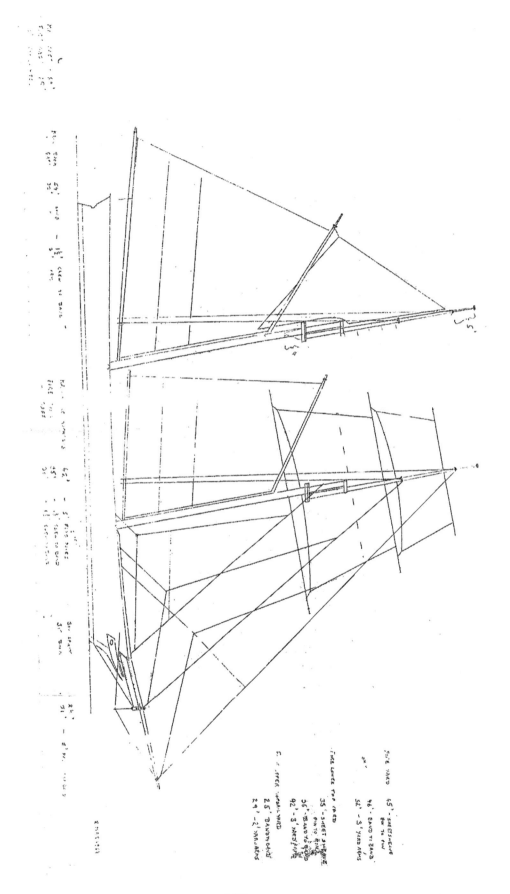

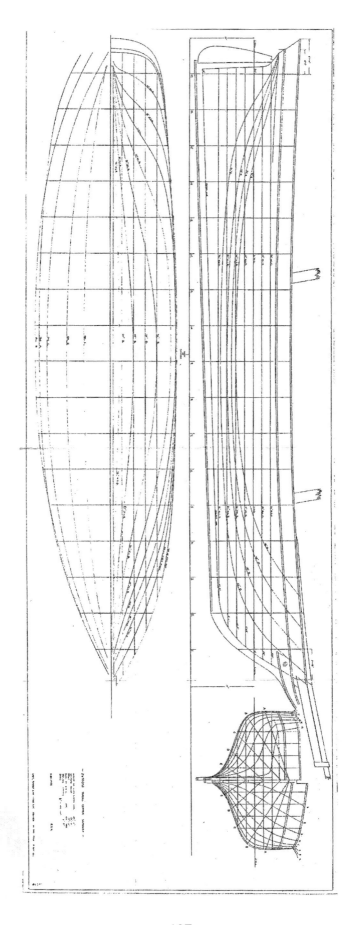

Made in the USA
Columbia, SC
20 November 2020